The Higher
Education of Women

*Published in cooperation with
The Higher Education Research Institute*

The Higher
Education of Women:

Essays in Honor of
Rosemary Park

edited by
Helen S. Astin and
Werner Z. Hirsch

 PRAEGER PUBLISHERS
Praeger Special Studies

New York   •   London   •   Sydney   •   Toronto

Library of Congress Cataloging in Publication Data

Main entry under title:

The Higher education of women.

    CONTENTS: Park, R. Some considerations on the higher education of women.--Raushenbush, E. Three women.--Kaplan, S. R. Women's education. [etc.]
    1. Higher education of women--Addresses, essays, lectures. I. Park, Rosemary. II. Astin, Helen S., 1932-   III. Hirsch, Werner Zvi, 1920-
LC1567.H53   376'.65   77-83486
ISBN 0-03-022301-6

PRAEGER PUBLISHERS, PRAEGER SPECIAL STUDIES
383 Madison Avenue, New York, N.Y., 10017, U.S.A.

Published in the United States of America in 1978
by Praeger Publishers,
A Division of Holt, Rinehart and Winston, CBS Inc.

89   038   987654321

To Rosemary Park

Preface
Helen S. Astin
Werner Z. Hirsch

This volume is dedicated to Rosemary Park, an admired colleague, respected woman leader, and eminent educator, and it contains contributions from a number of her close friends and colleagues. The idea to honor her in this manner originated at the time of her retirement, as she had inspired much admiration at UCLA as elsewhere previously. Together with Allan Carter, who participated until his untimely death in the editing of this volume, we felt that she had influenced higher education in America in a major way. A volume of essays and articles on a subject to which Rosemary has given much of her interest appeared therefore a suitable way to honor her.

To persuade Rosemary's former colleagues, friends, and admirers to contribute to this volume proved to be an easy task. That which binds the contributors together is a profound appreciation of Rosemary's vision and leadership in higher education, of her dedication to the values of scholarship, and of her intellect. She always has set her standards of personal conduct and scholarship at an unusually high level. Her discriminating taste for excellence in education and her complete devotion to its achievement--not lip service, but unwavering insistence--has made her a visionary. At the same time, her unusual insight into the workings of higher education and her ability to locate among many possible strategies the most powerful one for the circumstances, combined with her courage to fight for what she believes in, has often transformed vision into reality. As a consequence, she has always occupied an admired and somewhat unique position among university administrators. For Rosemary, working for a college or university in any administrative capacity has meant raising standards of achievement, deepening and broadening the reservoir of faculty talent, increasing the size of the library holdings and particularly of special collections, and introducing new art programs and museum acquisitions to solidly support them. Quality and not merely quantity has been her dominating concern at all times.

The volume is divided into three major parts. The first section includes an interview with Rosemary covering a number of topics that relate to the education of women, as well as to her own life and career development. The second section includes topics dealing with women's education and the status of academic women. Rosemary herself has contributed an outstanding historical perspective on the education and development of women. Esther Raushenbush provided a narrative account of the lives and contributions of three outstanding women leaders.

Since we were interested in an essay on the education of women at single-sex institutions, we asked Susan Kaplan, a student at Barnard College at the time Rosemary was president, to write on this topic. She contributed the chapter "Women's Education: The Case for the Single-Sex College." C. Robert Pace, a colleague at the UCLA Graduate School of Education, wrote "Liberal Arts Education and Women's Development." It was appropriate to follow this chapter with one that examines recent developments and innovations in curricula; Sheila Tobias prepared a thoughtful and informative chapter on women's studies. To satisfy interest in empirical information on women students in higher education, Alexander W. Astin wrote "The Undergraduate Woman."

The second section closes with two chapters, one by Margaret Gordon and Clark Kerr, "University Behavior and Policies," with special analyses of the status of academic women at Berkeley; and one by Helen S. Astin, "Factors Affecting Women's Scholarly Productivity."

The third part in the book presents some thoughtful policy recommendations with educational and social implications. The section opens with an essay by Hilde E. Hirsch and Werner Z. Hirsch, "Intellectual Quality: The Symbols and the Substance." The authors raise some critical questions about decisions by universities on the status of women and the reward structure. Alan Pifer and Avery Russell, in their essay, raise some important questions about affirmative action, discussing responsibility and public policy as a moral question. The section closes with an essay by Theodore M. Hesburgh. His brief account of the civil rights movement, leading into the women's movement, closes with his admiration for Rosemary, her contributions to higher education, and her stature as a dedicated woman leader.

This volume represents a celebration: Friends of Rosemary Park joined together to write on topics they wanted to include in a book dedicated to her. We hope that the volume will be read by young women who could be inspired by Rosemary's career and accomplishments. We also hope it will be read by policy makers to renew their regard for women's accomplishments and contributions to higher education.

We would like to thank Rosemary Park for inspiring us to write this volume. Milton Anastos' support throughout this effort is greatly appreciated. Thank you to all our friends, the contributing authors. We would also like to thank Beverly T. Watkins for her editorial assistance and Sally B. Anderson for keeping track of chapters, letters, and telephone calls from across the country, and for typing the manuscript.

Helen S. Astin and Werner Z. Hirsch

Contents

LIST OF TABLES AND FIGURES

Interview with Rosemary Park
Helen S. Astin

Q. I would like to ask you some general questions about women's education and women's status in academe as well as some personal questions about your own education and career development.

You are a very special person to a large and varied number of people. Students have the highest regard and admiration for you, colleagues seek out, respect, and trust your judgment. Friends enjoy your company enormously. Personally, I see you as an inspiration, a role model. Rosemary, could you tell me a little about the influences, factors that have been critical in your own educational choices and later on in your career?

A. I suppose the most important was the nature of the home in which I was brought up. Both my father and mother were university people. My mother had taught Greek and mathematics. My father was interested in higher mathematics as well as in languages. Our home was not a restrictive place. We all had a sense of independence--particularly a sense that neither of our parents was going to prescribe the kind of career with which we ought to identify. We soon learned that there were consequences from all of our decisions and I think that we tried perhaps to be somewhat more responsible and a little less experimental than we might have been, had we been sure that whatever we did there would be somebody there to catch us if we fell.

Q. Were you the oldest?

A. Yes, and this meant being told, "You were the oldest, you should have known better!" But actually, since my brother and sister were twins there were three of us who really made the team and then there was my little sister who had, I suspect, a rather more disciplined youth than we did because she had us to guide her as well as my father and mother--if I may use the word "guide" there in quotation marks.

Beside what went on in the home, I suppose I was very fortunate in attending good schools and in having teachers who were understanding and who encouraged me. I was very active in all sorts of student organizations at first. I was president of this and secretary of that. Somehow I had been convinced that it was important to try out all these things as well as being active in the classroom. When I went to college, I made up my mind that I had been active enough and then I began to really put my mind to studying.

Q. So the early leadership roles were during the high school years.

A. Yes, I was much more active in high school than in college. I always had good friends, but they were not necessarily interested in the things which concerned me. Perhaps having friends who were studying economics or music or classics gave me a somewhat broader background. I suppose it enabled me to contribute something to them as they contributed to me for we always treated each other with a great sense of independence.

Q. Can you talk about mentors; important people that played a mentoring role, or persons who served as role models for you?

A. I attended Radcliffe College, where the faculty were all Harvard faculty members, and therefore, all males. During my undergraduate years the president of Radcliffe was, for the first time, a woman. The academic dean was also a woman. But these people one didn't see unless there was a special problem so that I doubt that they were in any sense role models. I think we thought about our own futures without reference to their achievements.

Q. But do you remember, when you think back, in terms of your college years as an undergraduate and later as a graduate student, any special figures, professors, friends who played a mentoring role?

A. Possibly one assistant professor. He had traveled a great deal in Europe and I suppose was a kind of glamour figure for me because I was just a little girl from a suburb of Boston who had never been anywhere. To go into a classroom where you talked about who sang Sieglinde in the last performance in Munich or what restaurant one went to in Paris, this kind of thing, opened up a life which I could only imagine since it had no connection with my own existence. But I realized that this was a possible life and as a result I became more concerned with foreign literatures and cultures than I was with American studies. When I was in high school I had been very much interested in American history but once I went to college this closed, and only toward the end of my life did I return to a serious study of American problems.

Q. So these experiences as an undergraduate shaped your interests for graduate study?

A. Yes. My father had studied in Germany so that when I told him that I thought I would like to major in German in college he didn't dissuade me though he knew perfectly well that it would be difficult to get employment in this field. But, at the time I chose my major, employment was not my main concern. I was more concerned with the nature of the study itself.

Q. Yes, I was wondering if you thought in terms of making choices toward developing a career or did it just sort of happen?

A. I can quite honestly say I didn't think in terms of a career at all. If anybody had told me that I was preparing for the career that I eventually undertook, I would have been most surprised.

Q. So how did things develop?

A. Well, it was quite simple, actually. I was interested in studying. Though I took a Bachelor's degree in German I had never studied very much Medieval German. The summer after I took my B.A., Medieval German was offered in summer school which I attended. That naturally led me to studying some of the older dialects of German and to a Master's degree. One of the courses I took was given by a visiting professor from the University of Cologne. After I completed a piece of work for him, he said, "Why don't you turn this into a doctor's dissertation and come to Cologne where I am professor? It wouldn't take you more than a year and a half or two years to finish a doctorate." This I wanted very much to do but in the meantime, my father thought that it would be useful for me to get some kind of teaching experience and I eventually had a chance to take a class for two or three months. I taught in a girl's secondary school in Boston. In the afternoons after I finished teaching I continued studying for my doctorate. I enjoyed teaching very much, though I had never intended to be a teacher, but I realized that I needed a doctorate to advance in the field.

Q. Then when you completed, you returned to this country?

A. When I completed the doctorate in Germany it was March; there were no jobs when I came back nor were there any jobs in the following year. Again I was dependent on my family. My father at that time was president of a college and found me a part-time job in the German department. There had been an overregistration and they needed someone to help and so I was asked to take the position.

Q. So, he was your mentor in some ways--he was taking care of you.

A. He was very much there, though his career was quite as casual in its planning as mine. He ended up as a college president and had never intended to go that path any more, I think, than I had.

Q. So you saw yourself more as a teacher and scholar and then you moved into administration.

A. I moved into administration because really there were no jobs in teaching. I finally got a position, almost full-time, because someone died during the summer and Connecticut College needed someone to teach German that September. After two or three years of less than full-time teaching the college asked me to be Dean of Freshmen. I had had some experience with student advising in my father's college and when asked to undertake it at Connecticut I found it quite congenial. I continued my teaching even though this meant a very, very heavy schedule. As a consequence I didn't get ahead with publishing as one should at the completion of the doctorate. I had two articles accepted but there was never the opportunity to pull together the beginnings those articles represented. I soon found myself being shunted, without objection, into more and more administrative work. I served on all the main committees of the college and eventually I was asked to be the Academic Dean of the college while continuing to teach.

Q. So you really found yourself caught between the two--teaching and administration--all along?

A. I was almost always doing both.

Q. Now if you had to plan it a little differently, would you have liked for a while not to have had the administrative responsibilities and concentrate on some of your scholarly interests and writing?

A. Well, it might have been true. It was really difficult to say in what field or what area of Germanic studies I might have concentrated. I think I was happy that I had a balanced responsibility in which I had the respect of my colleagues because I did have to perform in the classroom and at the same time I knew more about the management of the institution than most of them did. It was for me a very good combination.

Q. When you were at Connecticut College you were instrumental in turning that college toward coeducation. What prompted you to invite men to participate as students at Connecticut College for Women?

A. Perhaps it's important to know that the men were invited to enroll in Master's degree programs, they were not asked to enroll for the Bachelor's degree. This came about because the college was neighbor to a number of scientific installations around the city of New London; the Pfizer Chemical Company and the Electric Boat Company are two examples. There were other small firms, all of which employed a good number of young scientists. These scientists couldn't really advance in their profession unless they could study further. At that time we had a number of very gifted young scientists on our faculty and they had begun discussions with these companies. The suggestion came then from the faculty that we offer a Master's degree to men as we were already doing for women. The presence of men in the classes in science, we felt, would have a good effect on the women. In those days there was a kind of folklore that women didn't do very well in either science or mathematics and that tended to be a self-fulfilling diagnosis. Anything that could make the women's study of these two subjects more serious would be an advantage. The enrollment of committed young male scientists in our classes might contribute to this result. So, without very much difficulty, we were able to charter Connecticut College for Men, which had the same Board of Trustees as Connecticut College for Women.

Q. Then, the Connecticut College for Women and the Connecticut College for Men coexisted at the same time?

A. We simply changed hats in the Board meeting and became the other corporation. At the time I was there, the college had the power to give degrees to men, but chose only to offer the M.A. Since that time the college has decided to grant the B.A. degree as well as the M.A. degree to men, so that the institution now is quite coeducational.

Q. What do you think about the Barnard and Columbia situation now? Do you have some feelings about whether Barnard should remain a separate entity as it has been or merge with Columbia?

A. I think that they are so closely merged in actuality that it may be good to preserve a little independence by maintaining the separate corporations. There were always differences in the teaching methods between the two institutions and in the offerings of the various departments. This added, I think, to the richness of the educational experience for both Columbia and Barnard students. There were difficulties, of course, then as now. Most of them, as I remember, were matters of personal difference rather than of educational philosophy. Columbia was never quite sure that it wanted an independent women's college; it would have preferred to manage everything itself. For instance, I was asked at one time not to go ahead with plans for the completion of a modern science laboratory for Barnard on the basis that Columbia had facilities. But I was uncertain whether Barnard would have any influence in the assignment of these facilities. In addition I thought the college should not seem to the public to say that it didn't believe in science for women since it did not provide its own laboratories but sent all its students to Columbia for science education. I always hoped that Columbia with its greater prestige would assist Barnard in enticing or inviting first rate faculty members. Barnard did not offer advanced degrees and it was important for distinguished people to know that if they joined the Barnard faculty they could offer graduate work in the Columbia faculties. There was, however, reluctance on the part of Columbia to help Barnard in the recruitment problem. Even today I would prefer to see increased cooperation from two separate entities so that there could be more experimental work than will exist if it's a totally centralized institution.

Q. Taking off from this last point you've made, could you elaborate on the issue of coeducation versus women's colleges today? What would be best for women's education?

A. I've experienced both types as a student and as a faculty member and I conclude that the matter of coeducation is primarily one of individual taste. Until the position of women in western society is somewhat more clarified, there is an advantage for certain types of women in having a home base where their problems take precedence. The women's colleges have met this responsibility for many years, in giving women a sense of what I would call cultural independence. I would, therefore, be sorry to see all women's colleges disappear. By the same token I imagine that this sense of home base will be less necessary. If the total society supports a greater equality of aspiration between the sexes in social and economic life, then perhaps one will not need this early experience of independence to make a successful life for a woman. I don't answer your question directly because I think it depends on the way society evolves in the next decades.

Q. But for the time being, as long as women have a need for a home base and a need for support and opportunities to explore without being threatened and intimidated, you would say that we do need the women's colleges?

A. Yes, I think this is particularly important for girls who develop slowly and we all have our own personal rates of development. To plunge a girl, uncertain about her capacities and aspirations, into a situation of great competition, not only intellectual where she must adjust to a kind of study in college which she has not been used to before, and then complicate that by great competition between the sexes I think is unfortunate. There are, of course, women who are quite capable of taking this on and for them the co-educational institution can be a very rewarding place. I would like to see both types of colleges continue. It seems a little ironic, I suppose, that nobody talks about defending the existence of the all-male institution. Apparently we don't feel that the boys need this kind of support as much as the girls. There may be some men who would benefit from the same kind of protective environment so that they could take their time in developing their own interests without the competition or distraction of the other sex.

Q. I would agree with you. One can project that the same principles, the kinds of threats that the young people might experience as they begin to relate to one another, could interfere for the boys as well as for the women.

A. The development of sexuality at that age is such a marvelous, exciting, and yet threatening kind of experience that a single-sex institution may offer a greater chance for maturity in dealing with sex in spite of the degree of unreality it represents. I lived in the women's colleges at a time when you were denigrated if you couldn't attract a man from at least 300 miles away for a weekend. The weekend culture of those years was a very unreal situation. There was kind of a romance about the distant prince or princess which the boy or girl whom you saw every day could not match.

Q. Continuing along the same lines, I have two more questions. One has to do with the contribution of women to higher education and the second has to do with the obstacles that women face in higher education.

A. Let me treat the contributions and obstacles from the faculty point of view. I have known some of the great faculty women from the early half of the century who were older than I, of course, and who had made their reputations on the basis of the work which they produced. No quarter was asked or given. They were recognized as first-class scholars irrespective of sex. It was generally conceded among them that you had to be better than the man but that was the way it was and you went about your business because you liked your business and you wanted to find the answer to the problem that you had posed. Whether this involved competition with a man was incidental, at least in the circles I knew. There were obstacles, of course. Indeed, these women in many cases were not paid anything like the salary that the comparable men were getting. That kind of discrimination existed and the women were conscious of it; if they discussed it it was usually explained by the fact that the men for the most part were married and had children. Some of the women, of course, were responsible for older relatives. On the administrative side, the only jobs open to women were in the women's colleges, with some rare exceptions. At Columbia occasionally, at the University of Wisconsin occasionally, a woman would rise to be head of a department but this was quite unusual.

Q. Was there a feeling of loneliness for the women, not having enough support systems, or being alone?

A. I really can't answer that. The women I knew were in love with what they were doing and had developed a life style around this which was highly satisfactory to them. I frankly don't remember them complaining about loneliness or not having support because they normally were the center of a group of younger people, sometimes men and sometimes women. They were known as scholars and admired for that.

Q. This brings me to a question I have; it is a personal question, but also I think it is important for women in general. As I understand, you remained single for quite some time and this was more of a tradition earlier, chosen by many academic women. Even today we are talking about it and I think how can we resolve and deal with the duality, the multiple roles that we have to juggle? How do you feel about it? How was it then, and what do you think and feel now for the young women aspiring to move into demanding positions along the lines you have pursued?

A. Well, I remember Millicent McIntosh who was my predecessor at Barnard saying that the single woman doesn't know what she is missing and therefore is less unhappy than she might be if she had some idea of what married life could be. I think this is very true. Again, it depends on what your perception of the given is. If the given is that you are quite fulfilled in the kind of life that you are leading as a single person then that's the kind of life you choose and continue to choose. I married someone very congenial in all intellectual and social matters so that it was not a great wrench for me to adjust myself to a new life style. It was simply an enlargement of a style that I was already used to living. One has to face, I think, the difference between casual relationships, which may have a great deal to contribute in some circumstances, and a more prolonged relationship. This is again a matter of temperament and not one to be generalized about. One makes one's choice in these things. If I had married younger and had had a family I think this would have really posed very great difficulties, even in the matter of physical energy. The management of a household today is complicated by the difficulty of getting adequate assistance. In the old, old days as I remember my mother's family, we always had two people at least in the house who assisted with the children but this is not possible today. If the woman has the physical stamina and the mental alertness to assume professional and home responsibilities I think it's a rich and wonderful life. If she doesn't have those energies then she has to limit the scope of her life. This again is a personal decision.

Q. Looking back into your own life again, what would you say have been the major satisfactions, challenges, pressures, and frustrations? This is a very large question.

A. One of the most interesting things was the attempt to bring modern dance into the curriculum of a college for women. No doubt it was easier to do this at a college for women than it would have been at a college for men. But when a school of modern dance was established at Connecticut College, one of the older members of the Board of Trustees whose ancestry went back to the American Revolution told me that it was the worst thing that I could have possibly done for the college. And I lived to see him make the motion in the same Board of Trustees to approve the budget of that school for the following year. In other words, he was open-minded once he had to face the existence, but he would never in theory believe that a school of modern dance could contribute anything to the education of young women or young men. The acquaintance with creative artists, their dedication and accomplishment were tremendously important not only for the students of the college but I think for the faculty as well.

Another time I was part of an effort to establish a discipline code during the years of student unrest at the University of California. We went the path of utter legalism which was acceptable to the students then who felt that their testimony was not given equal

weight in decisions with that of faculty or administrators. Though
students accepted the code and tried to make it work, the faculty,
who had an important role in the process, were not supportive.
Since then, a great many changes have taken place in student interests, in student behavior, and in student morale, so that this tri-
partite responsibility for the management of an aspect of university
life, which was the premise on which we built this system, has not
been sustained. The students have gone back to being students again
rather than aspiring to be full participants in the management of the
institution. In any case it was a most rewarding and important experience for me and I think had some benefits for the institution.

At the University of California, too, I had a part in encouraging a great many experimental courses. Some were so experimental that I was doubtful that they could succeed and in many
cases they didn't. Occasionally I was wrong and they did. But to
experiment with different approaches toward the learning process
which is what went on in most of these courses was a very exciting
thing to experience. While one discovered that the enthusiasm of
faculty and students for these new approaches was of limited dura-
tion, out of those years of experimentation came some greater under-
standings of subject matter areas that the university might treat.
I'm not sure that we learned anything that we couldn't have known
before but there was some merit in learning it in your own way, for
the institution as well as for the students and faculty who took part.

Q. Rosemary, you are an outstanding woman leader in higher
education. Looking at the leadership provided by women compared
to men in higher education, can you describe some special talents
that women bring to higher education? Also, think of yourself,
some of your own strengths and talents that you brought to this area.

A. I don't see myself in this leadership role. In the administrative responsibilities which I've had it was largely a question of
trying to broker a number of interests, one of which I eventually
came to feel was the one I personally wished to advance. But I
seldom was the person who had the insight first and then went out
and sold it to the followers, so to speak. My experience was that
in the course of dealing with an actual situation a number of points
of view would arise. As these were discussed positions were developed which could be shared with others. I suppose one must have
some capacities for expression to perform even that kind of brokerage role. I may have had that gift. Certainly I have always tried to
listen carefully when people speak to me and to discern to what extent their words are an accurate reflection of what they intend. One
can be very wrong in these matters but with time one does cultivate
a certain quality of perception and I have had many years of practice. I never saw myself as someone like Robert Hutchins with a

persistent point of view passionately maintained over years. I have always been concerned lest the intellectual side of education be misinterpreted and neglected. I have worried that we do not demand as much of students as they would willingly give us because we have misunderstood what they were asking of us. I have been therefore closer to the faculty in my administrative work than to the Trustees, although I've had my share of money raising and was involved in two big capital funds campaigns during which I went all over the country trying to raise money. Many of my experiences in that field would make lively cocktail conversation.

Q. Going back to the earlier conversation when I asked you about the challenges and the excitements, you did talk about creating. There were ideas you promoted, rather than play a mere brokerage role; I would say that in a sense you did play both roles. You brought leadership, you played a brokerage role, and also you raised funds.

A. There has to be some support from the group and my experience was that patience had a great deal to do with providing leadership. When a new curriculum is presented to the faculty, for instance, it usually loses the first time it comes to a vote. If you wait and still support the plan, within two or three years it will come back as a faculty suggestion and pass. Everyone feels he has had a part in it though you knew, of course, that it had started long before. This is a kind of sagacity, I suppose, and patience and faith that the idea is sound, as with the school of dance. Similarly, there were some fundamental changes in the Barnard curriculum when I was there. Though I was very much identified with these changes I always had a faculty group that either had come up with the idea in the first place or who supported it very wholeheartedly. Where one didn't have that kind of interest, one let the project drop. For instance, I thought that Barnard was a good place to hold weekend classes for women. The husbands were home over the weekend; they could take care of the children for several hours and the women could come to Barnard Saturday morning. With an occasional week or so in the summer, a good deal of college credit could be earned. I tried this out on the Barnard faculty and there was absolutely no support.

Q. When did you do that?

A. Oh, that was shortly after I went to Barnard; I had not fully realized that the Barnard faculty didn't live close to the college. They, perhaps rightly, felt that commuting for five days in the week was enough.

Q. The idea was very appropriate at the time regarding continuing education for women.

A. Yes, the idea was good and Barnard was an excellent place to do it, right in the center of New York City. There was the question of how large an audience would come and where the faculty would be found.

Q. In some ways the environment was good for the clientele, but not for the faculty who would have to commute and make a commitment.

A. Yes, this was true. Now, if there had been a greater interest, as I look back now, it seems to me that the college might have made some adjustments. If the regular program required three courses of the faculty possibly they could have carried two courses if they taught on Saturday. It could have been worked out. But when there was no response, then there were so many things one had to do that one said, let this one wait. And of course its time came later.

Q. As you see your life at this point, what lies ahead, what would you like to do?

A. There are many things. I think that if I were starting out again and if I had the right gifts I would go into science. It seems to me that this is where the excitement is and I wish that I had been directed into that field. That's why I hope that we thoroughly live down this feeling that women can't do mathematics and science which is a folklore largely restricted to America. I would encourage every woman today to make this a field in which she is at home. I would encourage women also to develop language capabilities. Indeed, I hope that the whole educational system in this country will begin to pay attention to bilingualism. In this part of the country, for instance, it is ridiculous that children are brought up not knowing Spanish. Having some interest in another culture is fundamental today. In America we seem to have retreated again into a single language culture from which we shall have to be sprung by drastic events as in World War II and then we shall probably be asking ourselves why didn't we learn more than English.

Q. It would be nice, I agree. You talked about the science and mathematics. You wished in some way that you had looked into it and had developed a knowledge and expertise, but you have so many other talents. As I asked you earlier, what would you like to do with your life now? What are some of the excitements you see ahead for you?

A. There are whole new fields of interest which have developed out of my marriage. I knew very little about the Classics, I knew nothing about Numismatics and this is a whole new area about which I look forward to learning more. It is an endless field, which involves fine arts as well as language and history. In public affairs the whole area of ecology concerns me. I serve now on a California Council for Economic and Environmental Balance in which it becomes apparent how desperately lacking we are in data and evidence in order to formulate public policy in these areas. The country doesn't know what its oil reserves are, the government doesn't know. This is an impossible situation in which to work out sound public policy. In the field of education I see a tremendous threat to private institutions and one has to keep asking, do they really contribute to a total national pattern and is the contribution so important that they should be continued under some new kind of government support? Can they be independent and still enjoy such aid? I see no reason why a system cannot be devised to provide it. We exist now in a mixed economy in which the private sector is weakening. We may now be, indeed, at the end of a development in economics and politics which has produced the most extraordinary luxury and security that any race of people has ever known. If we are approaching the conclusion of that development then a new form is coming which may mean greater governmental concentration of power in order to produce security.

Q. What would you advise a young woman starting her undergraduate career now?

A. I think the first thing I would say is to take this experience of study seriously. It is the one time in her life when the selfish cultivation of her capacities is the greatest social contribution she can make whether she is already in college or still in secondary school. So much of our later education tends towards highly specialized activities that one never finds out the full range of one's own abilities unless one tests oneself in those early years. So, I would say do not regard the school and college years as offering unimportant experiences. All forms of new experience contribute something to one's life. The problem is that there are dangers as well as opportunities attached. One can't tell ahead of time whether one is going to be adequate. Many times I have had a chance to do something quite different and new and I've said to myself, oh, I am so comfortable this way and things are going well, why should I disturb myself to go to Turkey, for instance. I knew nothing about Turkey and I was asked to go out there to evaluate an American college which had been there for a hundred years. To get enough background so that I could make some reasonable judgments about that institution in that particular environment was a very important experience for me. Indeed, I can't be grateful enough that I almost literally forced myself to undertake it. It's possible that forcing oneself to experience things is something which becomes more necessary as one grows older. When one is young the capacity for experience is more natural. But later one does have to make conscious decisions to embark on a new course and too often personal comfort may prove decisive. I welcome all sorts of new experiences provided that one has some capacity to come to grips with novelty. Of course,

there are always consequences from these experiences and I suppose
one's degree of maturity is measured by the ability to recognize the
fact that there are consequences. When one is very young there is
always someone there to pick you up. As one gets older there won't
be anybody there and you have to decide how you are going to get up
yourself. But I still say one should experience as many different
aspects of life as one can.

Q. It sounds like you're saying, "be very serious in what you
are taking but also enjoy it and have fun."

A. Enjoy it and have fun, yes. And find the things that give
you pleasure. Dare to say I am what I am and I don't have to find
pleasure in the things which other people enjoy. It's not a negative
judgment on me that I, for instance, do not like to play cards. As
a girl I had to go to card parties where I suffered acutely and I am
so happy that I have the courage to refuse today.

Q. What are some of the things you like to do for fun?

A. I love to go to museums. In any city I go to I always
search out the museum as soon as I finish my job and I have had
endless hours of greatest enjoyment. I like to read. I like to read
history, serious books; I'm not so good with contemporary fiction,
but I think that's a matter of age. I lose my interest unless it's a
very stylized kind of production. I love to travel, almost anywhere.
I suppose it stirs up the mind because there are adjustments to be
made and one discovers that one has a great deal of resilience and
flexibility. And exposure to new scenes and landscapes is very important to me. I like good food, which is something that I was not
brought up to.

Q. I asked you earlier what would you advise for undergraduate women; what would you advise a 45-year-old woman professor,
like me?

A. The danger of middle age is that one has developed blind-
ers, as you know, for the horse, so that he can't see what's on
either side of the road but only can see straight ahead. I would
rather have the horse see what was going on around him even though
he may not be making as much speed ahead. There need to be other
experiences which will supplement the professional experience and
give breadth to it. One should look into the area of aesthetics, or
other intellectual fields, or find ways to associate with groups of
people whom one might otherwise never know. That was one of the
good things about fundraising. One was always trying to explain
one's own profession to people who had no interest in it and you
desperately wanted them to have an interest and to show it. That
kind of activity engaged me at about the age of 45 and it proved a
most useful and salutory education for me, something which enlarged my concept of the professional.

Q. It's a great advice but it's so hard to do. One finds one's life at this point with enormous commitments in what one is doing, and one doesn't take a look back and say, well, I have another 20 years and I can relax. You think that you have to finish everything now. You don't allow yourself any leisure or experience in things other than writing, research, and teaching.

A. When you are wrapped up in a profession it takes almost every ounce of energy and you don't look ahead 20 years and discern that possibly the profession is going to change so tremendously in those 20 years that your contribution to it will become minimal unless you have a way of supplementing the professional capacities that you presently have. Therefore, just to protect that investment in professional excellence may require that you force yourself to know other things, even outside your field.

Q. It is interesting that even on sabbaticals, that supposedly have been built to help us along this way, we manage to overcrowd ourselves with the same things.

A. Yes, one of the problems is the lack of definition of what the sabbatical is supposed to do. The general public believes that the college professor doesn't work very hard, but the majority of them, especially today, work tremendously hard in order to keep up with ever expanding fields. This means that the attempt to maintain first-class professional standing is apt to take all the energy one has. This fact then needs somehow to be consciously circumvented. How you make the decision as to what the supplementary interest is going to be is very difficult. I used to be very interested in music especially when I was a student in Germany. That experience and my enthusiasm for fine arts were very helpful to me when for instance I was involved in setting up the school of modern dance. My avocational interest in history proved immensely useful, too, when I became a professor of education--something I never expected to be. This is how strange life is. And maybe this is the message, that it is strange and you can't see ahead, but you have to be open to it and welcome what is new and what keeps you off base.

Q. That's very good advice.

A. As I look back, I think the last and most important thought I have about what I've experienced is that, in my life at least, each year has been more rewarding than the one before. No one really quite believes that this can be true in a human life but I can honestly say that I have always found the next year more exciting and richer than the one before. I hope it will go on being this way.

Q. That's what makes you very special.

PART I

1

Some Considerations on the Higher Education of Women

Rosemary Park

Any account of the higher education of women must confront
the question of why the implementation of this sensible concept was
so long delayed. A brief examination shows that until the nineteenth
century frustration, not achievement, had characterized the history
of the idea. Though it was never a mass movement, the collegiate
education of women has always had proponents who have spoken loud
and well, but seldom, it would appear, in a completely convincing
fashion. The times were never right, no matter how propitious
they may have seemed to some.

One explanation for the enigma may be that the claim for
women's higher education was intertwined at most moments in history with other social issues and was seldom argued as a separate
cause. In religion it has been associated with various heretical
movements, in social history with different types of abolition, and
in politics with claims for suffrage. In most cases, the other issue
was resolved, and feminine education was postponed sine die. One
can only conclude that the idea of educating women disturbed the accepted wisdom of succeeding epochs more profoundly than is readily
apparent. Indeed, one historian can speak of the complete failure
of education in its more than thousand-year history to face the sexual
division of the human race (Ballauf 1969, vol. 1, p. 36). It may
therefore be useful to examine, even if only briefly, some of the
complexities which have attended attempts to encourage the higher
education of women.

As early as the latter part of the fourth century B.C. Plato
was insisting in the Republic and again in the Laws, the work of his
old age, that women and men were of the same nature and should be
subject to the same kind of education and nurture. In the Laws he
goes so far as to affirm that "nothing can be more absurd than the
practice which prevails in our country of men and women not following the same pursuits with all their strength and with one mind, for
thus the state, instead of being a whole, is reduced to a half" (Laws

VII, 805). No legislator, he says, should permit "the female sex to live softly and waste money and have no order of life while he takes the utmost care of the male sex . . ." (Laws VII, 806). A man's whole energy throughout life should be devoted to the acquisition of the virtue proper to a man, but this moral striving "applies equally to men and women, old and young" (Laws VI, 770).

Earlier, in the Republic, Plato had asserted that if the principal difference between the sexes lies in the fact that women bear children and men beget them, then "this does not amount to a proof that a woman differs from a man in respect of the sort of education she should receive" (Republic V, 454). This judgment prepares for his conclusion that "the same education which makes a man a good guardian will make a woman a good guardian; for their original nature is the same" (Republic V, 456). Of course, Plato was speaking here and in the Laws about an ideal community and not in any sense as an analyst of his own times, whose social and economic structure depended upon the institution of slavery. Nevertheless, it is significant that in his vision of a more just and better society, Plato could hold that it was in the best interests of the state that men and women should be equally educated to virtue and to participation in leadership. We know that the Greeks recognized the achievements of exceptional women like Sappho or Aspasia, or like Penelope and Alcestis in literary tradition. But for most Greek women life was restricted and education beyond reach.

Among the Romans there was initially little modification of the restrictions placed on women in Greek society. In general Roman law did not permit women to own property outright or to have ultimate control over their children. They were subject to easy divorce by their husbands on a variety of grounds. Nevertheless there emerged in Rome as in ancient Greece women who were distinguished for their learning and influence. Both the Greek and Roman pantheons, in the early days of those societies, paid tribute to Athena or Minerva as the goddess of the intellectual side of human life as well as to her as counselor and patroness of the arts and industry. To neither Greeks nor Romans did it appear incongruous, it seems, to associate intellectuality with feminine attributes.

By the time of the late Republic, it was being observed that most prominent families had their "startling women," as one critic puts it (Balsdon 1962, p. 15). Many of these extraordinary types, like Pompey's wife and Brutus's, had been well educated. Both these ladies were conversant with Greek and mathematics, and the latter was even known as the "philosopheress." Ovid, in the Art of Love, suggested that women be well instructed, particularly in the classics, so that their conversation might be more sprightly. During the Empire distinguished women appeared at banquets and other public functions. Roman matrons played an important economic role in the city's life. The emergence of women poets, the political skill and power of some of the emperors' wives, and other feminine achievements have led critics to suggest that a kind of equality of the sexes at the highest social level was on its way during the Empire, despite the strict provisions of the laws (Rengstorf 1954, p. 16 note). Honorific titles such as mater patriae, mater castrorum, consors regni (Vogelsang 1954, pp. 4-5) or the epithet docta puella (Balsdon 1962, p. 56), were not unusual.

In spite of these indications of recognition for feminine capacities Roman society never moved to establish general educational opportunity for women at more than the elementary level except for unusual women of the higher rank. In part this neglect may be explained by the early marriage age, which left little time for learning before household responsibilities were assumed. A contributing factor may have been the increasing interest in the ascetic cults and mystery religions of the late Empire, which tended to cultivate the irrational aspect of experience, for which education in the liberal arts was not necessary.

Prominent among these philosophic movements was Neoplatonism, one of whose last great representatives was the woman philosopher, Hypatia of Alexandria, brutally murdered in 415 A.D. Descended from Plato, Neoplatonism initially emphasized the attainment of insight through the discipline of such rational studies as mathematics and logic. Becoming increasingly mystical in the fourth century, it came to interpret the physical body as a clog upon the soul, and, therefore, encouraged an ascetic view of life. This attitude was even more pronounced among the proto-Christian hermits of the Egyptian desert, reports of whose saintly lives were brought to Rome by Athanasius in 339 or 340 A.D. (Grützmacher 1969, vol. 1, pp. 226-27). He told of men and women living in Egypt, often as anchorites, under discipline and in strictest continence. The effect of these reports was to move a number of prominent Roman matrons to attempt a similar ascetic withdrawal in order to foster deeper religious insight. A generation later St. Jerome, who had himself experienced this desert life from 373 to 379 A.D., arrived in Rome to testify to the spiritual merits of this ascetic withdrawal.

EARLY CHRISTIAN VIEWS

In its Christian form the cultivation of ascetic practices was to extend down to the present day and, since it combined in its origins many different traditions, its history is correspondingly complicated. Beginning with the Gospel accounts it appears that, unlike

the society into which he was born, Jesus treated women with understanding of their aspiration to equal participation. His visit to the
home of Martha and Mary was as nonconforming as was the presence
of women at his expositions of the Law (Leipoldt 1955, p. 125).
Neither of the actions would have been countenanced by the somewhat
primitive Palestinian community. They explain, however, the
presence in the earliest Christian communities of women as prominent members who in some instances appear to have taught and ex-
pounded the new doctrine. Priscilla, whose conversion of Apollos
is described in the Book of Acts (18:26), is a distinguished example.
According to the Gospel of Mark women were present at the death of
Christ. And it was to Mary Magdalene that Christ first appeared
after the Resurrection (Mark 16:9). Though the Bible records this
early prominence of women and their later missionary and minister-
ing activities, no status commensurate with these contributions
seems to have been accorded them in the later Christian church.
It was apparently not the Gospel account which came to determine
women's relationship to the new religion, but rather the interpretation of St. Paul, which combines aspects of the mores of the Palestinian community with the revelation of the Gospels and ascetic principles very similar to those formulated by the Neoplatonists later on.

On the status of women, St. Paul's statements are not unam-
biguous. Almost as revolutionary as Plato's are his words in Galatians 3:28, ". . . there is neither male nor female: for ye are all
one in Christ Jesus." But they must be balanced against 1 Corinthians
14:34, where he writes, "Let your women keep silence in the churches:
for it is not permitted unto them to speak; but they are commanded to
be under obedience, as also saith the law." But Paul also writes
about women praying and prophesying in the churches (1 Corinthians
11:5) and requires certain men to be silent there (1 Corinthians
14:28). The need to keep order in the church services is sometimes
adduced as the reason for this commandment to silence on the part
of all women and of some men. Paul's preference for continence,
"But if they cannot contain, let them marry: for it is better to marry
than to burn" (1 Corinthians 7:9) should perhaps be understood in
connection with his remark later on in the same chapter (1 Corinthians 7:29), that "the time is short." The eschatological atmosphere of early Christianity could be interpreted to mean that, since
the world is about to come to an end, one should not be bothered with
familial responsibilities. But there are other passages that reflect
more clearly an unwillingness to give women an equal place in the
establishment of the new community (Ephesians 5:22-24; Colossians
3:18; 1 Timothy 2:11, 12; 1 Peter 3:1-5).

Some explanation for refusing women full participation in the
Church can be found in the fact that, during the early days of Chris-

tianity, it was necessary to distinguish sharply between Christians and pagans. In many heathen rites women, like the sibyls in Greece and the vestal virgins in Rome, took part as priestesses. Similarly, among the heretical Christian sects such as the Montanists in the second century and the Marcionists, who persisted in some form from the second century until the seventh or even later, women were permitted to perform ecclesiastical functions. One way, therefore, for the orthodox Christians to make clear the difference between themselves and the heretics or the pagans was to impose restrictions upon the role women might play in the Church. When a special priestly class developed within Christianity itself, in spite of Tertullian's statement "omnes sacerdotes, quia sacerdotes nos Deo et Patri fecit" ("all are priests since he made us priests for God and the Father." Tertullian, De Monogamia, p. 1247. 13-14), the cadre was limited to males. Women served as deaconesses or belonged to a special group called the widows, to whom certain functions were assigned, in connection with baptism, for instance. But the participation of women was more restricted as the Church grew. Among the heretical sects, however, the apocryphal and heretical texts show that "startling women" emerged who continued to prophesy and to convert others, as in the early days of Christianity. Such women were Thecla, the daughters of Philip, Febronia, Xanthippe, Polyxena, Marianne, Helen and, among the heretics, Maximilla, Prisca, and Philomene. In light of the achievements of these women, it is interesting to speculate on the effect on the status of women that might have ensued had the heretics and pagans rather than the Christians limited the extent to which women might participate in the ritual.

When the church fathers in the second, third, and fourth centuries came to develop the official position of the Church on women, they tended to found it upon the Old Testament account of the creation and the fall. Eve and the ancient word for serpent were said to have a common root in Hebrew. More important was the fact that God had created Eve second, assigning her a lower order of significance and indicating that she had not been created in the image of God, as man had been. Eve's act in tempting man to sin was the essence of enmity toward God and led, in later times, to lengthy argumentation on whether indeed woman had a soul at all. Through her sin sexuality was imposed on the human race and woman was perceived as the embodiment of this sexuality, which was interpreted as Satan's way of continuing the temptation of man. Women were described by the Fathers as "the door of Hell," "the stirrup of Satan," or, as Basil said, "a beast of many wiles having the garb of a sheep" (Thraede, Patrologia Greca [PG], pp. 256-57). Ambrose's judgment, "Per mulierem stultitia, per virginem sapientia" ("Through woman came

folly, through the Virgin wisdom") (Thraede, p. 257), though referring to the Virgin Mary, was nevertheless characteristic of the
conditions under which woman and intellect might coincide. It would
appear from these negative judgments that the mores of the ancient
Near East communities, where Christianity originated and where
there was little respect for the average woman, played the controlling role in defining the early Church's attitude toward women.

Even the movement toward the middle of the fifth century to
glorify the Virgin Mary as Theotokos (she who bore God) did not
modify this position fundamentally. The intent of the Councils of
Ephesus (431 A.D.) and Chalcedon (451 A.D.) in decreeing the title
of Theotokos for the Virgin was primarily to document more amply
the divinity and manhood of Christ. The word used to describe the
Virgin's function is workshop (ergasterion). Proclus, bishop of
Cyzicus, whose sermon in the Great Church at Constantinople is included in the Acts of the Council of Ephesus, proclaimed that Mary
was the "workshop" in which the two natures were welded together
(Acta, p. 103). Earlier the same word was used by St. Epiphanius
when he too referred to the Virgin as the workshop in which the
Saviour effected our salvation (Migne, PG, 43, 88D). As the cult
of Maryolatry developed in the later centuries the Virgin Mary, of
course, became the recipient of worship in her own right and assumed increasingly feminine qualities. Even this evolution from a
workshop to a loving Mother came too late to modify the secondary
position formally assigned most other women in society. The Virgin
was the greatest of the exceptional women in history, but her eleva-
tion into a special category of regard did little to change society's
estimate of the rest of the sex.

Though most of the church fathers accepted this traditional
attitude of repression toward women and none ever expressed any
confidence in their general capacities as Plato had, nevertheless
they were often in their personal lives associated with devout and
learned women. This was particularly true of St. Jerome, who attacked women savagely in his tract, Adversus Iovinianum, but who
was the center of a group of intellectual women in Rome to whom he
offered instruction in Hebrew and explication of scriptural texts.
Marcella, Paula, and Eustochium, though of different generations,
were the recipients of his letters and his interest. Origen in the
third century dedicated his treatise on prayer to Tatiana; in the
fourth century Ambrose shared his scholarly activities with his wife
Marcella. His younger contemporary St. Augustine in the last book
of his Confessions (XIII) noted that woman's share of rational intelligence is equal to man's, though she remains subject to the sex of
her husband (Augustine, p. 465, see also p. 435).

Beyond these individual relationships, the Church itself
achieved spiritual distinction through the many early Christian martyrs it honored among whom were many women. At the end of the
patristic age the opportunity to redefine woman's role which might
have emerged from Jesus's teaching failed to come to fruition. Instead a few extraordinary women were noted and glorified, while the
rest were suspected of being Satan's tools unless they vowed continence or devoted themselves to good works.

THE MONASTIC MOVEMENT

With the institutionalization of asceticism in the West in the
monastic movement, convents were founded for women who sought to
pursue the virtues of chastity and charity in the religious life. From
the sixth century on women also came to these cloisters not only to
escape unwanted marriages or the heavy hand of paternal authority,
but because these retreats offered them an opportunity for education.
The names of some of the great abbesses, learned in their own right,
have come down to us: Radegunda of Poitiers, Brigit of Kildare,
and Hilde of Whitby. The most outstanding feminine scholar in the
early Middle Ages was, no doubt, the nun Rotswitha of Gandersheim.
She was acquainted with most of the Latin classics, Virgil, Horace,
Ovid, Terence, and Plautus, as well as with the works of Christian
writers. Fearful lest the sisters should be corrupted by reading
secular texts, she composed, among other works, a series of dramas
based on Terence, though, as she said, "avoiding the wicked passion
of illicit love" and "the tempting talk of the amorous" (Eckenstein
1963, p. 168). Her works indicate the high degree of education which
some women attained within the cloister.

In the twelfth century, however, the dangers of educating
women were demonstrated only too clearly in the tragic tale of
Heloise and Abelard. Heloise was the niece of a canon who had encouraged her studies so that, as Abelard himself said, "in literary
excellence she was the first. And as the gift of letters is rare among
women, so it had gained favor for her and made her the most renowned woman in the whole kingdom" (Muckle 1964, p. 26). Attracted by her learning and beauty, Abelard seduced and secretly
married her. She eventually overcame her passion for him and entered the religious life, where she achieved great eminence. As an
abbess she was admired by St. Bernard and Peter the Venerable,
but the qualities which they praised were her spirit of religion, her
prudence, and her meekness. After her fall no further mention was
made of the distinction of her mind, and it would appear that her
learning was viewed only as a source of pride which had to be overcome if she were to attain the Christian virtues proper to a woman.

For men in the monastery the study of the liturgy itself developed scholarly skills and interests. Such concerns were less open and relevant to women, since they did not participate in the liturgical aspects of the church. Though the standards of learning were initially quite high in the convents, by the fourteenth century they had sunk considerably (Power 1975, pp. 80-81). Female instructors, however, began to appear outside the cloister by the end of the century (p. 83). As from the beginning of the Christian era, women attained eminence in the medieval heresies as they had in earlier variants from orthodoxy. Eileen Power suggests that this was because women were dissatisfied with the role assigned them within the medieval church and state (p. 30).

For some women, however, the phenomenon of chivalry and courtly love must have provided an escape from the heavy demands of medieval householding or the alternative discipline of the cloister. The perfect knight chose his lady and served her often in secret, without any assured hope that his loyalty would be rewarded by worldly intimacies. Like the status accorded the Mother of God, these courtly ladies in the great game of chivalry were elevated above the mass of women, and perfect chastity and charity were attributed to them, at least in literature. They served as an inspiration to art and letters and to courtly behavior, thereby increasing woman's responsibility for the refinement of manners and morals. Some great ladies of the chivalric romances had acquired literate skills. Isolde could read and write several languages, Blanchefleur shared the instruction given to Flore, and Lavinia wrote Aeneas's name on a wax tablet. But these attainments were quite secondary to their beauty and their charm. In general, learning was associated only with the clergy and not with all of them in those times. As early as the sixth century Theodoric's daughter was forbidden to have her son instructed by a grammarian, lest such learning rob him of the common soldier's respect (Weinhold 1897, vol. 1, pp. 114, 115, 119, 121, 130). In chivalric times, much the same attitude persisted.

EUROPEAN HUMANISTIC REVIVAL

Not until the humanistic revivals in western Europe did learning become respectable for men again, particularly for those outside the Church. Then the worldly culture of the royal courts, with international marriages arranged in dynastic interests, required both men and women of the upper classes to be competent in modern languages and in Latin, which was the lingua franca of the time. Queen Elizabeth I of England spoke French, Italian, Spanish, and Flemish. Latin and Greek she mastered so well that she translated from those languages for pleasure all her life. Her tutor, Roger Ascham, relates that he once called on Elizabeth's relative, Lady Jane Grey (later to be the nine-day queen), and found her reading Plato's Phaedo in Greek, while the rest of the court had gone hunting. Erasmus's letters contain descriptions of the household of his good friend, Sir Thomas More, each member of which read and studied the liberal arts. More's daughter, Margaret Roper, was renowned for her proficiency in Latin and Greek, as well as in music and the sciences. His other daughters were equally skilled, and it was the achievement of these women which led Erasmus to a favorable attitude toward the higher education of women (Erasmus to William Budaeus, p. 575). When he composed Utopia More, like Plato, provided that both men and women in his ideal community should devote a certain amount of time to study.

In his comments on More's household, Erasmus, besides noting the devotion to learning common to all members, observed that their chief concern was piety. This combination of learning and piety was recommended as the best educational program for women by the Spanish humanist Johan Loys Vives, who acceded to the request of Catherine of Aragon and developed a plan of female education especially designed for the Princess Mary, Elizabeth's older half-sister. In his dedication, Vives wrote to Queen Catherine that he was moved to the task "partly by the holiness and goodness of your living, partly by the favor and love that your Grace beareth toward holy study and learning" (Vives 1541, London, p. ii). Both Erasmus and Vives viewed learning as a means to virtue for women. This suggestion, though reminiscent of the Socratic tenet that virtue is knowledge, reflects a concern for combating the idleness and frivolity of the upper classes rather than a genuine wish to advance female scholarship. Vives specifically stressed the need to avoid what his sixteenth-century French translator called "livres damnables" (p. 43), which corrupt good manners and female minds. Instead, women should read the lives of the saints, Boethius's Consolation of Philosophy, and the works of the church fathers.

This trend of thought is familiar in other contemporary tracts on female education. One published in London in 1598, entitled On the Necessarie, Fit and Convenient Education of a Yong Gentlewoman, urged that woman be dissuaded "from al that might impech and hinder her mind fro the augementation of her vertue" (W.P.). The author concluded by urging, "Let the small profit got by learning be compared with the great hurt that may happen to them" and suggested that the reputation of "a grave and honest matron" was to be preferred to "the book and pen with an uncertaine report." Clearly, only certain kinds of learning were conducive to virtue, and virtue was apt to be synonymous with chastity. At all cost, the amorous

and impudent verses or fables of men like Boccaccio were to be
avoided. These are like music, which "openeth the gate to many
vices."

The same general sentiments on women's education appeared
again in a similar tract a century later by one T. D. entitled The
Excellent Woman, Described by Her True Characters and Their Opposites and published in London in 1692. The theme was clearly
stated: "As Vertue is as much more worth than Knowledge; the
Ladies ought to think that 'tis of more avail to them to be good than
learned" (p. 23). Nevertheless, as the author pursued the subject,
he began to defend the further education of women with considerable
warmth: "Whatever can be said, they (women) are capable of these
(arts and sciences) as well as the Men; and if they quit sometimes
what they might pretend to, this is more out of Modesty or Consideration than out of Weakness" (p. 138).

These sentiments were repeated with even greater force by
Mary Astell both in her work Some Reflections Upon Marriage (1696),
dedicated to Queen Anne, and in her study, A Serious Proposal to the
Ladies for the Advancement of Their True and Greatest Interest
(1697). Her theme appeared early in the latter: "Women are from
their very Infancy debar'd those Advantages with the want of which
they are afterwards reproached" (1697, vol. 1, p. 16). Like her
predecessors she assumed that, "It is Ignorance, either habitual or
actual which is the cause of all sin" (p. 19). Neither the heart nor
the will suffice for virtue "if the Understanding be Ignorant and
Cloudy" (pp. 32-33). She proposed a kind of women's college for
the nurture of their minds and the service of God (p. 37), believing
that such an institution would help "to stock the Kingdom with pious
and prudent Ladies whose good Example--will so influence the rest
of their Sex that Women may no longer pass for those little useless
and impertinent Animals which the ill conduct of too many has caused
'em to be mistaken for" (pp. 43-44). There is a long way indeed between the condemnation by the church fathers of women as the doors
of hell and this moderate description of them as "impertinent Animals." More important is the proposal that the weaknesses of
women, moral and intellectual, could indeed be overcome through
education, since "God has given Women as well as Men intelligent
souls" (p. 47).

As men's colleges had found some women donors to advance
their educational programs, why, Mary Astell asked, should there
not be found women who would contribute to establish a college for
women? She presented her plan to Queen Anne, who thought well of
it until she was dissuaded by Bishop Burnet. It was to the same
bishop that Mary Astell's friend Mary Wortley (later Mary Wortley
Montagu), wrote in 1710 requesting him to comment upon her translation of Epictetus.

> My sex is usually forbid studys of this Nature and
> Folly reckon'd so much our proper Sphere, we are
> sooner pardon'd any excesses of that, than the least
> pretentions to reading or Good Sense. We are per-
> mitted no Books but such as tend to the weakening and
> Effeminating the Mind, our Natural Deffects are every
> way indulg'd and 'tis look'd upon as in a degree Crim-
> inal to improve our Reason, or fancy we have any. . . .
> (Montagu, p. 44)

A more eloquent case for the further education of women could hardly be made. But neither Mary Astell's proposal nor the example of Mary Wortley Montagu's intellectual attainments was sufficient to overcome the resistance to granting women the educational opportunities open to men. The fear that women would be corrupted by too much education and that education would merely make them more wiley and subtle tools of Satan persisted even into the Age of the Enlightenment. Indeed the noted French bishop of Orléans, Monseigneur Dupanloup, called by the Pope apostolus juventutis, was to remark in the mid-nineteenth century that "the predjudice against the cultivation of the intellect in women is one of the most culpable notions of the 18th century" (Dupanloup, p. 26).

ATTITUDES IN COLONIAL AMERICA

This same prejudice thrived in America as part of the cultural baggage which came with the Puritans to Massachusetts Bay in 1630. Many of the first settlers in that group were university men, but since the universities were not open to women (although they were the object on occasion of feminine benefactions) there was little reason to expect a different attitude among the colonists. Perhaps there was though, if one remembers the deep fear of reversion to barbarism and the great concern which the Reformation brought to the careful examination of the sources of Christian conviction. In the wilderness the need to perpetuate a learned clergy and respect for letters soon called forth the founding of Harvard College (1636), one of whose avowed purposes was to develop in the laity a secure knowledge of the arguments for their faith. To achieve this end each household was expected to be a center for Bible reading and study under the direction of the husband and father. Though St. Paul was not mentioned, 1 Corinthians (14:35) described the practice of the colony: "And if they [women] will learn anything, let them ask their husbands at home." It is noteworthy nonetheless that in the overwhelming task of maintaining orthodoxy women were not more directly enlisted, even if it had been necessary to give them a more careful education in order to prepare them for this mission. Some explanation for the failure of the colonists to do so can, perhaps, be deduced from the comments made by John Winthrop, first governor of the colony, on his first wife's letters.

> When I considered of suche lettres as my wife had written to me and observed the scribblinge hande, the mean congruitye, the false orthog., and broken sentences etc.: and yet founde my heart not onely acceptinge of them but delighting in them and esteeminge them above farre more curious workmanship in an other and all from hence, that I loved hir. (Winthrop, vol. 1, p. 106)

He married her in 1605 and she bore him six children before her death in 1615 at the age of 32. To an extent, then, the early marriage age and the number of children, both at home and in the colony, explain the lack of time for female instruction. Indeed the annual population increase in Massachusetts Bay between 1690 and 1780 reached as high as 28 percent, even excluding immigration (Cremin 1970, p. 481).

Elementary education, of course, was a concern of the General Court, which as early as 1647 had ordered every township with 50 households to provide a teacher "to teach all such as shall resort to him to write and read" (quoted by Cremin, p. 181). If a township had 100 households, it was required to establish a grammar school with a master "being able to instruct youth so far as they may be fitted for the University" (quoted by Cremin, p. 182). Though no sex distinctions were made in these laws, it is clear that only boys were meant for the university preparatory course, since the word youth then as now could be used to refer explicitly to males. Whatever individual families might do for their daughters, the community concerned itself only with the education of men.

This predilection was no doubt further enforced by the great tremor which Anne Hutchinson's heresy sent through the colony in its early days, and to which the Quaker women who came to the colony in the hope of making converts contributed. Women seemed to have a weakness for heresy and were therefore not reliable in doctrinal matters. Most of the Salem witches were women. But education was not considered to be a remedy for these deviationist tendencies. Even Thomas Jefferson, who once spoke of woman's natural equality (Jefferson, p. 211), did not urge his own daughters or other women to seek higher education except as a provision against boredom: "A plan of female education has never been a subject of systematic contemplation with me" (p. 687).

There were, however, other Americans who found the matter one for contemplation and action. Anthony Benezet, a Quaker of Huguenot descent, urged the establishment of a school for girls in Philadelphia, where he began to teach in 1754 and returned after acquiring experience in the instruction of poor children, particularly of Negroes. His was a limited, if genuine, vision for youth. Study has a tendency, he wrote, "to raise their minds above that simplicity of heart and manners to which we as a people, in divine favor, have been called" (Brookes 1937, p. 389). His other comments reflected a fear that education would, if pursued too far, prove dangerous and undermine the necessary sense of one's place in the fitness of things.

In the more revolutionary circle of the Adams family, a different sense of proprieties developed. Abigail, wife of John Adams, the second president, had never been to school herself, but throughout her correspondence with her husband over the many years of separation entailed by his diplomatic responsibilities, she urged fairer educational opportunity for women. Writing to him in the crucial days of 1776, she said, "I long to hear that you have declared an independency--and by the way in the new Code of Laws which I suppose it will be necessary for you to make, I desire you would remember the Ladies and be more generous and favorable to them than your ancestors" (Adams 1875, p. 149). To this petition John Adams replied, "As to your extraordinary Code of Laws, I cannot but laugh" (p. 155). It did not occur to him or to Jefferson that, in a sense, their new American society was assigning woman a place without representation, exactly as in the old country. Adams and Jefferson both held that the education of the two sexes should be different, but they were not deeply concerned about the content of female education.

Nevertheless it would appear that Adams was relying upon his wife to educate their children and firmly believed, as he told her, that "it should be your care, therefore, and mine, to elevate the minds of our children and exalt their courage" (p. 119), without questioning the source of this capacity in her. He even ignored her reproach when she wrote, "If you complain of neglect of education in sons, what shall I say with regard to daughters who every day experience the want of it? With regard to the education of my own children, I find myself soon out of my depth, destitute and deficient in every part of education" (p. 213). It is easy to imagine the mingled bitterness and eloquence with which she urged that the new Constitution encourage learning and virtue: "If we mean to have heroes, statesmen and philosophers, we should have learned women" (p. 213). Like other distinguished men of his time, Adams no doubt believed that women could be prepared before marriage by some

experience in the community and by correction in the home, to become the competent women whom de Tocqueville on his travels in
America was so much to admire. "If I were asked," wrote the
Frenchman in 1835, "to what the singular prosperity and growing
strength of that people ought mainly to be attributed, I should reply,
'To the superiority of their women'" (de Tocqueville, vol. 2, p. 225).
This superiority consisted in their possession of great delicacy in
personal appearance though they had "the hearts and minds of men"
(p. 223).

These qualities, however, do not seem to have been recognized
by Charles Francis Adams, Abigail's grandson, who when writing of
her life in 1875, could say that Abigail's ideas, or at least some of
them, were romantic illusions, the product of a rather solitary childhood devoted to reading (Adams 1875, pp. xi-xii). Nor did Charles
Francis Adams share de Tocqueville's prediction that, just as social
changes were bringing father and son, master and servant, and
superiors and inferiors closer, so these changes were making woman
more and more the equal of man (de Tocqueville, vol. 2, p. 222).
Instead Mr. Adams closed his memoir on his grandmother's life by
observing sententiously: "However keenly women may think or feel,
there is seldom an occasion when the sphere of their exertions can
with propriety be extended much beyond the domestic hearth or the
social circle. Exactly here are they to be seen most in their glory"
(Adams 1875, p. xxii).

For at least a generation women had extended their activities
beyond the domestic hearth, for example, the girl millhands in the
Lowell textile mills--where women in 1831 constituted 80 percent of
the operatives (Lemons 1973, p. 20)--or the many women school
teachers throughout the country. But Mr. Adams apparently was not
aware of these statistics or the speech on slavery delivered before
the Massachusetts legislature in 1838 by Angelina Grimke (who was
the first woman to address that body), or the election in 1848 of
Maria Mitchell, the astronomer, to the American Academy of Arts
and Sciences, founded by his grandfather in Boston, or the M.D. degree conferred upon Elizabeth Blackwell by Geneva Medical College
in 1849. Nor did he take notice of the statement made in 1848 by
that interesting collection of men and women in Seneca Falls, N.Y.,
which resolved "that it is the duty of the women of this country to
secure to themselves their sacred right to the elective franchise"
(O'Neill 1969a, p. 111). This was a right to which John Quincy
Adams apparently had given some thought when he responded to the
charge that he should not present petitions from women to the Congress, since they had no right to vote, by asking, "Is it so clear
that they have no such right. . .? (quoted by Flexner 1974, pp. 47-
48; but see also J. Q. Adams, Memoirs, vol. 10, p. 37). In 1868

the women's suffrage amendment was first presented to Congress
(Flexner, p. 173). By 1850, women constituted 24 percent of the
manufacturing labor force of the country (Flexner, p. 78), and by
1870 women workers were organizing nationally (O'Neill 1969b, p.
102). Though these were all signposts to a different future, Charles
Francis Adams was not the only one who negated them or interpreted
them as serious aberrations. Nowhere can this narrow attitude be
studied better than in the final, successful struggles for women's
higher education which took place during his lifetime.

Among the millhands in the Lowell textile mills in 1835 was a
young woman named Lucy Larcom, who later gained fame in New
England as a poet. At the age of 11 she entered the mill as an em-
ployee along with other girls from the area, and so was typical of
the young women who were seeking employment outside the home in
some socially approved form. School teaching and millwork were
the two respectable occupations that were open. But teaching required education, which was difficult for a poor girl to secure. To
remedy this lack another New England lady, Mary Lyon, had been
seeking funds to found a women's college, as Mary Astell at the beginning of the eighteenth century had tried in vain to do. Mary
Lyon's program, which began in 1837, was to prepare "young ladies
of mature minds for active usefulness, especially to become teachers" (Goodsell 1931, p. 254). "We hope," the officials of the new
school announced, "to redeem from waste a great amount of precious
time, of noble intellect and of moral force" (p. 275). The attribution
of these qualities to women was unusual, particularly in light of the
Biblical and patriotic tradition. What had changed was the outside
world, which now called into action characteristics of women formerly unperceived through the theological and cultural haze.

ECONOMIC AND POLITICAL PRESSURES

From the very beginning it had been clear that an educated
citizenry was essential to preserve the political form. As the
economy began to expand with the opening of the West and the population continued to increase, the need for trained men became more
urgent. Teachers were in short supply and the teaching profession
was unpopular, largely because men preferred to take advantage of
the many other more lucrative kinds of employment which then
abounded. Catherine Beecher estimated in 1853 that the country
was short at least 60,000 teachers (American Woman's Educational
Association [AWEA], p. 13). Women, however, if trained, were
immediately available and would work for less than men. Mabel
Newcomer summarized the situation by saying, ". . . it was becom-

ing increasingly apparent that the only way to get even a minimum universal education for male voters was to employ women teachers" (Newcomer 1959, p. 15). It was not therefore the arguments for women's education on the grounds of fairness or equality which prevailed at the midcentury, but ironically the economic and political need of the country, which nevertheless continued to exclude most women from political and economic decisions.

Though the training of teachers was the proximate cause, Mary Lyon's program sought fundamentally to mold and exploit the moral force of women which, she implied, society had wasted until then. Actually, history did not attribute such a quality to most women. Only the great exceptions, the Virgin, the Martyrs, and the Romantic heroines, were perceived as sources of moral strength. Now the achievement of a few was deemed to be characteristic of the sex as a whole. The evolution is difficult to follow in its successive states and requires a much more careful analysis than can be given here, if the philosophical, social, and educational motivations and implications are to be considered. But some factors in the change can be mentioned.

The new assessment of women was not confined to America. Indeed, the Romantic movement at the beginning of the century had already presented such a type, the most compelling expression of which is to be found in the final chorus of Goethe's Faust, "Das Ewig-Weibliche zieht uns hinan" ("The eternal-feminine draws us on"). This eternal feminine was not the result of learning, as the sixteenth century might have held, but was founded rather on Shaftesbury's notion of a moral sense. The Victorians also believed a gift of this sort was particularly strong in some women. The Romantic poets had used the category of the beautiful soul, for whom goodness was not the result of the will but innate and exercised naturally. Mary Lyon and others tried to focus this moral sense upon the needs of the community, working particularly through the church and the schools. More radical and perhaps more gifted women than Mary Lyon were active in other areas, for example, the Grimke sisters and Harriet Beecher Stowe in the struggle against slavery, and Frances Willard in the crusade for temperance. In these reform movements and in the organized demand for women's suffrage, women became associated in the public mind with virtuous but perhaps visionary attempts to influence public policy. Conservative critics tended to feel safer if women stayed at home, where their moral sense could exercise a beneficent influence upon their children and husbands. From this point of view, women's education should obviously confine itself to the familial aspects of life.

Catherine Beecher (1800-78), who was a sister of Harriet Beecher Stowe and daughter of Lyman Beecher, descended from an original founder of the New Haven colony, was particularly effective in developing plans to this end. Brought up in the shadow of an angry Puritan God, she gradually freed herself from that stern theology to formulate a code of ethics in which individual conscience, not pervasive fear of divine punishment, was the basis for morality. Conscience, she held, was developed in the family, and this hypothesis led her to assign women the primary role in maintaining the moral standards of society (Sklar 1973). Through her influence the American Woman's Educational Association was formed in 1852 and sought to create a liberal profession for women by establishing permanently endowed institutions which would offer programs in the particular business of women. This was defined as presiding over women's special space, the home, mastering the care of the human body, understanding the nature of the human mind, particularly in its initial stages of development, and, in general, being responsible for the conservation of the family state (AWEA 1853). Such an education would prepare women for marriage or for teaching. This ingenious idea offered some education to women and served at the same time to enhance domesticity, which the well established middle class preferred to the more public life of the upper class.

Beecher assumed that most women would marry or become teachers, and that for these good women the education she proposed would prove useful. But there were, of course, other women of whom it could not be said that they were good. At any rate, their innate goodness was in eclipse and they were viewed as direct descendants of the temptress Eve and likely tools of Satan. Unlike the good women who were thought to experience no sexual pleasure in the male embrace, these other women could feign a pleasure they might not feel and, because of this art or capacity, were an attractive temptation to men. It was widely conceded, indeed, that many men required such relationships in addition to marriage, and so the double standard flourished. On the one side was the chaste good woman protecting the home and on the other the less fortunate, unprotected woman who embodied all the worst judgments of the church fathers on the female sex. The ethical situation resulting from the double standard and the consequent uneasy conscience of men produced a glorification of the home and the good woman, while the prostitute was left to whatever social agencies might exist. Amelioration of her lot was believed to depend on strengthening her will and her religious faith. Only later in the century were other factors, like the absence of apprentice programs for girls, the disruption caused by urban development, and the destitution accompanying large-scale immigration regarded as contributing causes of the widespread prostitution of the time.

In these circumstances, any attempt to suggest an increase in activities for women outside the home was suspect. It was this kind of concern that made the role of the first proponents of the higher education of women so difficult. Mary Lyon in her efforts was attempting to show that a life prescribed and limited by men's admiration for the good woman did not require or challenge her total capacities. Mary Lyon's college, Mt. Holyoke, was intended for those "whose great desire is to be prepared to use all their talents in behalf of the cause of education and of the Redeemer's kingdom" (Goodsell 1931, p. 281). These talents included intellect as well as moral power, and it was to the training and enhancement of both that the college directed its programs, with the intent of making women better wives, mothers, teachers, and "companions of men in their religious work" (pp. 237, 238). Collaboration with men and not the independence of women was Mary Lyon's aim. To be effective companions to men in the church and in the schools, women required comparable education, she concluded, and the courses at Mt. Holyoke therefore strongly resembled those at Amherst, a neighboring college for men. Ancient history, political science, natural philosophy, rhetoric, algebra, and logic were the topics of study which were to prepare women for greater usefulness.

There were other women, however, who were less interested in cooperative endeavors directed toward social betterment than in establishing an independent identity for women based on a more accurate assessment of their capacities. Such a woman was Margaret Fuller of Boston, whom Horace Greeley, her one-time employer, said was "the most remarkable and in some respects the greatest woman whom America has yet known" (Wade 1940, p. 143). "The intellect," she said, ". . . is not to be cultivated merely that woman be a more valuable companion to Man, but because the Power who gave a power by its mere existence signifies that it must be brought toward perfection" (p. 133). Through her writing and her conversation series, a kind of adult education course for Boston women, she tried to wean women away from what she called their "passionate sensibility" (p. 133) and toward a genuine development of intellectual interests as a part of a whole personality. In imitation of Margaret Fuller's educational efforts for women, Amelia Bloomer and Elizabeth Cady Stanton, both "startling women," set up in New York state a conversation club to examine the women's rights movement, especially as it related to employment and education. "It is the fault of education that she [woman] is now intellectually inferior," wrote Amelia Bloomer in 1851 in her newspaper, The Lily. "Give her the same advantages as men, throw open the door of our colleges and schools of science and bid her enter, teach her that she was created for a higher purpose than to be a parlor ornament or mere plaything for man. . . ." (Bloomer 1895, p. 63). Margaret Fuller had been dead a decade before these words found a sympathetic echo or a practical implementation.

In 1861, however, a retired Poughkeepsie brewer, Matthew Vassar, opened the first meeting of the board of trustees of the women's college he had just founded with the words, "It occurred to me that woman, having received from her creator the same intellectual constitution as man, has the same right as man to intellectual culture and development" (Newcomer 1959, p. 1). His statement did not emphasize the assistance trained women could bring to social betterment in collaboration with men, but rather asserted the importance to the individual woman of an education that developed her as a freestanding human being in relation to human culture. Ludicrous as it may seem, in this sentiment the Poughkeepsie brewer and the Athenian philosopher Plato were of one mind.

The same thought was repeated by Sophia Smith when she founded Smith College in 1875 "to furnish my sex means and facilities for education equal to those afforded now in our colleges for young men" (p. 55). Of particular significance is the statement in an early catalogue that, "The College is not intended to fit women for a particular sphere or profession but to perfect her intellect by the best methods which philosophy and experience suggest" (p. 55). To these policies an elderly Catherine Beecher responded with some disgruntlement by saying, "When I read the curriculum of Vassar and other female colleges, methinks their graduates by such a course as this will be as well prepared to nurse the sick, train servants, take charge of infants and manage all departments of the family state, as they would be to make and regulate chronometers or to build and drive steam engines" (Goodsell 1931, p. 203). Despite this judgment other women's colleges like Wellesley (1875), Radcliffe (1879), Bryn Mawr (1885), and Barnard (1889) all chose to follow Vassar and to offer women the same liberal education provided men, for whom it was antecedent to training for the established professions.

None of these were then open on equal terms to women, though women graduates were as well prepared as men to enter such programs. With a few exceptions, it would be more than a generation before the women's colleges could assure their students that the education they received would, like the comparable education of their brothers, prepare them for any professional instruction or activity.

The same frustration was encountered by the women graduates of the state universities and land-grant colleges. These institutions became coeducational at their founding or shortly afterwards. Most testified to the beneficent effect of the presence of women on the campus. "Sexual isolation for the purpose of culture," said President Welch of Iowa State Agricultural College in 1871, "is contrary to nature: it makes boys rough and girls silly" (Friends of Agricultural Education [FAE] 1967, p. 56). Perhaps more important was the fact that the girls proved capable of mastering calculus and meeting every other requirement that was made. "Some of our best scholars have been ladies," commented President Denison of Kansas Agricultural College at a meeting of the Friends of Agricultural Education in 1871 (p. 57). There was, however, a tendency in these institutions for girls to concentrate in home economics and education, while the boys studied engineering and agriculture (Newcomer 1959, pp. 90-91). These choices reflected the persistent idea of a special sex-typed learning for women, in which Catherine Beecher so vehemently believed and which sustained the concept of glamorous domesticity as the ideal state for women.

Strangely enough, this romantic assessment of women seems to have been the effective impetus for women's suffrage in the first states which granted women the vote. Except for certain local peculiarities, as in Utah with its Mormon population, it was what John Stuart Mill called "silly panegyrics on the moral nature of women" (Mill 1869, p. 77) which secured the vote for women and not their capacity to distinguish themselves in the liberal arts or to judge public issues dispassionately. The suffrage movement, of course, exploited both positions by claiming that women's moral sense would cleanse politics once they secured the vote and that women were as competent as men to understand political questions. It did not make an issue of higher education for women, perhaps because most, but not all, of the leaders had attended college (Kraditor 1965, p. 281). Indeed, women's colleges probably profited more from public interest in the campaign for women's suffrage than they actually contributed to it themselves.

Both movements, education and suffrage, were harassed by pseudoscientific predictions of failure and doom. The weight of the female brain, many pointed out, is actually less than that of the male; accordingly, higher education would involve acute and intolerable strain for women (Haller 1974, p. 37). Educated women would not marry (O'Neill 1969b, pp. 80, 81); therefore, the college presented a eugenic threat. "The vulgar poems of Chaucer or the amorous ditties of Burns or Byron" were likely to produce complications at the time of pregnancy or menopause (Haller, pp. 103-04). Since even the bicycle was held by some physicians to be immoral (p. 180), higher education and the vote were resisted as destructive of the good woman, whose moral sensitivities could only be weakened by forcing knowledge and public activity upon her. Despite these dire prophecies college education for women increased, and in 1920, more than 70 years after the Seneca Falls declaration of sentiment, the suffrage amendment was finally ratified.

CONTEMPORARY ATTITUDES

As the twentieth century advanced, however, it became clear that neither the fears nor the hopes for the higher education of women had been realized. Women proved they could leave the home to earn a livelihood or to study without suffering physical, mental, or moral collapse. In spite of women's extensive contributions to winning two world wars, most professions were effectively closed to them either on grounds of presumed incompetence or lack of interest and commitment. Nevertheless, the number of women gainfully employed increased steadily. In 1910, 23 percent of all females over ten years of age belonged in this category (E. K. Adams 1921, p. 21). By 1975, employed women constituted 30 percent of the total female population, and employed men represented 49 percent of the total male population. Women were most numerous among clerical workers. Only 5.2 percent of women employed in 1975 were designated by the Bureau of Labor Statistics as managers or administrators, compared with 14 percent of men employed (World Almanac 1977, p. 128). Except for teaching and nursing, both typed as feminine vocations, the other professions remained inhospitable to women.

The traditional objections to women's activities outside the home persisted in muted fashion. A great deterrent came from women themselves, who, particularly after World War II, preferred domestic life. Indeed, in those years the women who had fought for suffrage, which had been won in World War I though no man fought for it, as Carrie Chapman Catt said (Lemons 1973, p. 3), seemed slightly ridiculous to the younger generation. The wars had resulted in the collapse of empires and in the rise to power of the organized working class. So far as the settled middle class from which most women college students came was concerned, these revolutions were adequate, and there was no urge to press for a reassessment of the proper place of women, particularly since in America this group enjoyed the highest level of security and luxury any women had ever attained in history.

By 1959 the average age of women at first marriage had declined sharply to 20.2 years (Goode 1963, p. 47). Family size increased temporarily but, nevertheless, these women emerged from their childbearing years with 20 or 30 years ahead and no easy access to the labor market. The frustration of this group was described by Betty Friedan in The Feminine Mystique (1963). Now, for almost the first time, some middle-class women began to doubt whether life in the home was as fulfilling in the modern age as they had believed and whether their influence for good was as real and effective as society and tradition suggested. From this same middle

class came the student leaders of the peace and civil rights movements, to which was soon added an organized demand, in the rhetoric
of the time, for women's liberation. Though the arguments had been
made before, this time the disequilibrium of society, resulting from
other challenges, occasioned greater sensitivity and more receptive
concern for the woman question.

For a variety of reasons and coincidences, some of which
were related to the pressure of minorities for access to the leadership in society, legislation was passed by the Congress which, if
successfully enforced, would open the advanced professions and
their specialized training programs, as well as other positions of
community leadership, to the competition of women and minorities.
Thus today the state is nearer than at any other time since Plato to
profiting from the full capacities of its citizens instead of being reduced by half. It has taken until the close of the twentieth century to
complete in theory a social revolution which began in classical an-
tiquity. And it is not yet certain that the relation of the sexes to
each other and to their respective educations has been clearly perceived and securely established. Society, however, is less sure
that good women are as influential and as remote from biological
reality as the Victorians thought. We know that the standards of
society do not rest with these women alone but are the shared responsibility of the two sexes, both inside and outside the home. At
the same time, more women than ever before aspire to a full range
of social and economic choices, and this means a change in the traditional relations and tasks of the sexes.

Furthermore, higher education, which was once for the young,
is now open to all adults with a variety of forms and consequences.
Society itself is searching for new sources of authority and may well
begin to look to higher education for something in addition to expertise. At such a malleable time and in light of the qualities attributed to women in history, women's collegiate education is of
fundamental importance. Through it women can realize the claims
which legislation encourages them to make, since no one doubts that
women can learn anything men can learn. Whether they learn in
separate or coeducational environments is a matter of choice and of
temperament, rather than of program.

The more difficult question is whether society has finally overcome its doubts about the higher education of women and whether the
hopes Margaret Fuller had expressed at the beginning of the last century have been realized. "What woman needs," she said, "is not as
a woman to act or rule, but as a nature to grow, as an intellect to
discern, as a soul to live freely and unimpeded" (Howe 1883, p. 152).
Surely women are closer to this ideal today. If this brief history of
their desire for education teaches anything, it is how persistent and

varied are the negative assessments of women through the ages and how modest in consequence their aspirations. Though the revolution to permit women to enjoy what Thomas Jefferson once called "her natural equality" (Jefferson, p. 211) may not be over, a significant first stage has now been set in legislation. What men and women together in new lifestyles will make of this longed-for opportunity, only the future can tell.

REFERENCES

Acta Conciliorum oecumenicorum, tomus primus, volumen primum, pars prima (Concilium Universale Ephesenum, ed. Eduard Schwartz). Berlin, 1927. (For this and a number of other references I am indebted to my most compassionate and learned critic, Milton V. Anastos.)

Adams, E. K. Women Professional Workers. New York: Macmillan, 1921.

Adams, John and Abigail. The Familiar Letters of John Adams and His Wife Abigail, ed. C. F. Adams. (1875). Reprint. Freeport, New York: Books for Libraries Press, 1970.

Adams, John Quincy. John Quincy Adams, Memoirs, ed. C. F. Adams. vol. 10. Philadelphia: J. B. Lippincott, 1876.

American Woman's Educational Association (AWEA). First Annual Report. New York, 1853.

Astell, M. A Serious Proposal to the Ladies for the Advancement of Their True and Greatest Interest (in two parts). London, 1697.

Augustine. Confessions. Cambridge and London: Loeb Classical Library, 1977.

Ballauff, T. Pädagogik. Freiburg and Munich: Karl Alber Verlag, 1969.

Balsdon, J. P. V. D. Roman Women. London: Bodley Head, 1962.

Bloomer, D. C. Life and Writings of Amelia Bloomer. Boston: Arena Publishing Co., 1895.

Brookes, G. S. Friend Anthony Benezet. Philadelphia: University
    of Pennsylvania Press; London: H. Milford; Oxford University
    Press, 1937.

Cremin, L. A. American Education, the Colonial Experience,
    1607-1783. New York: Harper and Row, 1970.

Dupanloup, F. A. P. Studious Women. Translated by R. M.
    Phillimore. London: Virtue and Company, 1868.

Eckenstein, L. Woman under Monasticism. 1896. Reprint. New
    York: Russell & Russell, 1963.

Erasmus, D. Opus epistolarum Des. Erasmi Roterodami. Edited
    by P. S. Allen and H. M. Allen, Vol. 4. London: Oxford
    University Press, 1922.

Flexner, E. A Century of Struggle. New York: Atheneum, 1974.

Friedan, B. The Feminine Mystique. New York: W. W. Norton,
    1963.

Friends of Agricultural Education. An Early View of the Land-
    Grant Colleges. Urbana: University of Illinois Press, 1967.

Goode, W. J. World Revolution and Family Patterns. London:
    The Free Press of Glencoe, Collier-Macmillan, 1963.

Goodsell, W., ed. Pioneers of Women's Education in the United
    States: Emma Willard, Catherine Beecher, Mary Lyon. New
    York and London: McGraw-Hill, 1931.

Grützmacher, G. Hieronymus. Leipzig, 1901. Reprint (3 vols.).
    Aalen: Scientia, 1969.

Haller, J. S., and Haller, R. M. The Physician and Sexuality in
    Victorian America. Urbana: University of Illinois Press,
    1974.

Howe, J. W. Margaret Fuller. Boston: Roberts Brothers, 1883.

Jefferson, T. The Life and Selected Writings of Thomas Jefferson.
    Edited by A. Koch and W. Peden. New York: Random House,
    1944.

Kraditor, A. S. The Ideas of the Woman Suffrage Movement. New York: Columbia University Press, 1965.

Leipoldt, J. Die Frau in der antiken Welt und im Urchristentum. 2d ed. Leipzig: Koehler und Amelang, 1955.

Lemons, J. S. The Woman Citizen--Social Feminism in the 1920's. Urbana: University of Illinois Press, 1973.

Migne, J. P. Patrologia Graeca. Paris, various dates.

Mill, J. S. The Subjection of Women. 1869. Reprint. Cambridge: M.I.T. Press, 1970.

Montagu, M. W. The Complete Letters of Lady Mary Wortley Montagu. Vol. 1, edited by R. Halsband. Oxford: Clarendon Press, 1965.

Muckle, J. T. The Story of Abelards' Adversities (annotated translation of the Historia Calamitatum). Toronto: Pontificial Institute of Mediaeval Studies, 1964.

Newcomer, M. A Century of Higher Education for American Women. New York: Harper and Brothers, 1959.

O'Neill, W. L. The Woman Movement. London and New York: Allen and Unwin, Barnes and Noble, 1969a.

O'Neill, W. L. Everyone Was Brave: The Rise and Fall of Feminism in America. Chicago: Quadrangle Books, 1969b.

P. G. (Patrologia Graeca): See Migne.

Plato. The Dialogues of Plato. Translated by B. Jowett. New York: Random House, 1937.

Power, E. Medieval Women. Cambridge and New York: Cambridge University Press, 1975.

Rengstorf, K. H. Mann und Frau im Urchristentum. Cologne and Opladen: Westdeutscher Verlag, 1954.

Sklar, K. Catherine Beecher. New Haven: Yale University Press, 1973.

T. D. The Excellent Woman, Described by Her True Characters and Their Opposites. London, 1692.

Tertullian. De Monogamia, 12, 2 Corpus Christianorum, Series Latina 2, Tertulliani Opera 2. Turnholt: Brepols, 1954.

Thraede, K. In Reallexikon fur Antike und Christentum, S. V. Frau. Vol. 8, Lieferung 58, Stuttgart, 1970; quoting Basil, Patrologia Graeca 30, 820-21, and Ambrose, Corpus Christianorum, Series Latina 14, Ambrosii Mediolanensis Opera 4, 108, 89-90. Turnholt: Brepols, 1957.

de Tocqueville, A. Democracy in America. 2 Vols. New York: Random House, 1945.

Vives, J. L. A very Frutefull and Pleasant Boke called the Instruction of a Christen Woman. London, 1541.

Vives, J. L. Livre de l'Institution de la Femme Chrestienne. Translated by P. Changy. Havre: Lemale et cie., 1891.

Vogelsang, T. Die Frau als Herrscherin im höhen Mittelälter. Gottingen: Musterschmidt Wissenschäftlicher Verlag, 1954.

W. P. On the Necessarie, Fit and Convenient Education of a Yong Gentlewoman. 1598. Reprint. New York: Da Capo, 1969.

Wade, M. Margaret Fuller. New York: Viking, 1940.

Weinhold, K. Die Deutschen Frauen in dem Mittelälter. 3d ed. Vienna, 1897.

Winthrop, R. C. Life and Letters of John Winthrop. 1864-67. Reprint. New York: Da Capo, 1971.

World Almanac. New York: Newspaper Enterprise Association, Inc., 1977.

2
Three Women: Creators of Change
Esther Raushenbush

Higher education in America has been characterized by unparalleled growth and change. Out of the selective institutions designed during this country's early history to educate ministers, lawyers, and statesmen has grown an immense complex of institutions for an expanding population with expanding purposes: public and private, secular and sectarian, coeducational and single-sex institutions; land-grant universities; vocational and professional institutions; municipal colleges; colleges for black students; junior and community colleges.

This diverse development has also included the emergence of individual institutions, often small, created or recreated to meet new needs and, often, to point the way to change. These institutions provide opportunities impossible or unlikely in large and traditional colleges and universities. They are often the work of an individual or a small group prompted not only by an idea, but by a sense of mission.

This is an account of three women whose vision was largely responsible for the making or the remaking of three institutions, each marking a step in the evolution of higher education in the past half century. They are Clara Mayer of the New School for Social Research, Jacqueline Grennan of Webster College, and Lucy Sprague Mitchell of Bank Street College.

CLARA MAYER AND THE NEW SCHOOL
FOR SOCIAL RESEARCH: "Learning
has no age limit"

The New School for Social Research in New York was established with what is probably the most specific intellectual goal of any institution of higher education since colonial times and with the least official preparation. World War I, which was supposed to resolve major national and international problems and usher in an era of decision by reason instead of by war, taught the nation that the war would not itself accomplish these things but would instead add even more complex issues. A League of Nations, the search for peace-loving leaders, the extension of suffrage--everywhere there were right-minded people who attached themselves to one proposal or another for freeing the world from war and advancing the civilization of mankind.

America had always had faith in the power of education: an informed people would be a wise people. Now, in a catastrophically changed and changing world, it was more important than ever that intelligent people be provided with the information and the opportunity to inquire into critical issues, national and international. Education as we had known it would not do. A group of successful and sophisticated scholars decided the country needed a new kind of university, a university for intelligent adults who would give direct attention to the most important issues society faced.

Motivations were varied. Behind them all was the conviction that political and economic problems should be studied and attacked directly, and no institution in the country was doing that. Some of the most restless and innovative thinkers in the United States, then attached to traditional institutions, were dissatisfied with the way the educational bureaucracy had responded to the war and its aftermath, and this dissatisfaction spurred them to seek change. To some of them the London School of Economics, as described to them by Harold Laski, provided a model.

James Harvey Robinson and Charles Beard, deeply discouraged by affairs at Columbia University during and after the war, had often discussed establishing a new institution. Alvin Johnson, then editor of the New Republic, devised a radical plan for a new institution for adults (Johnson 1952), and Robinson and Beard left Columbia to give impetus and life to the plan. Wesley Mitchell and Thorstein Veblen joined them. Clara Mayer, a student in search of a teacher, followed Robinson immediately and from the beginning was central to the shaping of the institution that grew out of their combined efforts.

The distinguished group of educators who established the New School for Social Research were by no means agreed on the design of the new institution, but they were all sure that the school should be free of the bureaucratic demands of the traditional university. It was to have no credits, no degrees, a student body of self-motivated adults, and a faculty without hierarchy, interested in discussing with their students the critical social issues of the time. Nobody wanted a blueprint or an organizational chart; they wanted to open the school and they did. Johnson wrote later that "The New School opened with éclat for the spring term of 1919. Every liberal

in the city was excited by the novel venture of an institution headed
by two such dynamic figures as Robinson and Beard, self-defrocked
from the conventional academic life" (1952, p. 278). The school's
first announcement declared:

> In view of the difficult situation in which humanity finds
> itself, a group of men versed in the various branches of
> knowledge relating to mankind have drawn together for
> counsel . . . for the establishment of a center of in-
> struction and discussion . . . to seek an unbiased under-
> standing of the existing order . . . as well as those
> exigent circumstances which are making for its re-
> vision. (New School 1919).

Clara Mayer, just graduated from Barnard College, came for
this first session. She did not invent the New School, but she was in
at the birth, and she was to be a force that gave form and continuity
to a highly individualistic institution. It was she who helped make an
orchestra out of a band of solo players, guiding it through its difficult early years and on to a development that has no duplicate in the
country: an educational system with no traditional safeguards which
counted on high motivation in students and high talent in teachers to
create a freemoving undergraduate education for adults. Nothing
like it had ever existed.

> When I was a student at Barnard, a principal reason for
> wanting to be a senior was being able to take James
> Harvey Robinson's course in intellectual history. At
> least it was a principal reason for that group for whom
> college is a kind of turning point in life, a sudden con-
> sciousness of its possibilities and its hardships, of
> realities on a bewildering scale. The course was not
> a disappointment. I decided to take all the others he
> gave and found as time went on that I would have to
> take some of them downtown--he was about to change
> his classroom. Downtown was the New School.
>   That was pretty much the way he felt about it, or
> rather the way he hoped he might feel about it once he
> had made for himself--and for others who felt the
> same way--a school in which only the essentials of the
> intellectual life counted, that is, investigating freely,
> and teaching freely students who wanted to learn without
> hope of any additional reward in the form of credits,
> diplomas, or anything else. (Mayer)

Clara Mayer had completed her undergraduate education. She came to the New School as a student, but she was immediately engaged in administrative activities in an institution that had almost no administrative structure. From the beginning she was at the center of the educational activities of the school and was, for almost all of its first half century, the chief architect and conductor of its undergraduate program. When the school decided later to grant undergraduate degrees she continued in that role for the degree program and also for the noncredit program, which remains the heart of the institution.

The second year found the New School staffed by an illustrious faculty, drawn by the prestige of Robinson and Beard and the opportunity for professors to teach what they chose as they chose. They were teaching a growing number of interested students. The faculty, then and all through Clara Mayer's administrative life, included an extraordinary number of men and women important in the intellectual life of this and other countries.

As always the utopian ideal soon met unyielding realities, and the school was torn by dissension. People quarreled. The school lacked the support that more cautious institutions build before they commence operation. Faculty resigned, board members resigned, and many people judged that these few first years were all the New School would know.

Johnson, still editor of the New Republic, had so far taken little part in the activities of the school, but he was unwilling to see it die, so he took charge himself. For him the most encouraging sign of the school's relevance was students' insistence that it should continue. At the most discouraging moment of dissension, three students came to him and offered to help. Clara Mayer was one of the three. Johnson wrote later:

> They were confident that there were rich resources for
> the support of the school in the student body. They
> could not only recruit new students; they could also help
> in raising funds.
> The meeting gave my spirit a great lift. It had
> been my dream, from the time of the launching of the
> school, that the students should be enlisted not only for
> the promotion of the institution, but also for participa-
> tion in its government. (1952)

Even with the dislocation of that third year, the functions and style of the New School had been established. Distinguished teachers continued to want to teach there, and it was clear that the school was serving an increasing body of adults for whom the social science orientation of the first years was important.

To implement Johnson's plan that students should have an important part in the school's operation, he appointed Clara Mayer to the reconstituted board of trustees. She was then in a position to interpret the school to the other trustees. She became secretary to the board, and was soon the principal officer for appointing and inducting faculty and shaping the curriculum. By 1930 she was assistant director with Johnson, dean of the school of philosophy and, for the rest of her years there, codirector of the school.

In her second year she designed an informative catalogue that not only communicated the character of the New School but also described the point of view of the various lecturers and the content of their courses. This catalog which, through the years, has retained its original form, has been regarded nationally and internationally as a model for people and institutions interested in education as the New School conceived it.

Many of the characteristics of the New School that made conventional people look at it askance were indispensable qualities which, all through the changes of personnel and fortune, have never been abandoned. It was an open university with open admissions, for adults who had begun but knew they had not completed their education. If, without grades and credits, a student had insufficient motivation to continue a course or to study, that was his problem, not the school's. He could stay away, or not study. If the absence of a departmental structure meant that a field was incompletely covered, complete coverage was a responsibility the institution did not assume.

It did assume the responsibility to provide highly qualified teachers, working at the front edge of their disciplines, creating knowledge at the same time they were disseminating it to students who had no purpose in coming except to learn. Robinson's lectures of those years produced <u>Mind in the Making</u>. Gardner Murphy found the first forum for his discussion of parapsychology. Hanya Holm and Martha Graham taught dance in the school and carried on their performing life outside it. Writers taught students who wanted to write and wrote poetry and fiction and plays during their teaching years.

There were no department heads. Clara Mayer soon became the appointing officer and she was the principal educational association the faculty had with the school, other than the students.

The New School grew. Circumstances and imagination created new tasks for it. As time went on it responded to new demands. Students who were not interested in credits and degrees continued to come in large numbers, but others who wanted to work in the educational style of the New School needed a B.A. degree or credits they could transfer to other institutions. For them, the school became accredited, but it continued to give major attention to those who wanted an education and were not interested in degrees. These noncredit students have always been at the forefront of the school's attention; they were never looked on as second-class citizens, as they are in many places. Such students were always central to Clara Mayer's attention and interest. She was indefatigable in her search for intellectually exciting courses and teachers for them. Credit and noncredit students attended the same classes. The school established a rule that credit students would do required assignments and attend an additional discussion section to which noncredit students would not be admitted. But when a teacher took exception to this and said he wanted interested noncredit students to attend the extra sessions Dean Mayer immediately agreed and the rule was ignored.

The principal professional interest of the people who started the school was in the social sciences. They were determined that education should address itself to the catastrophic problems the twentieth century was facing. Clara Mayer thought beyond this: one of the earliest curricular expansions she fostered was the teaching of psychoanalysis and psychology. This began in the early 1920s.

The explosive effect of the development of psychoanalysis in Europe was repeated in this country when the great disciples and colleagues of Sigmund Freud came to America. From the first they were engaged to teach at the New School. About this development Miss Mayer wrote:

> The School's founders were concerned with what they
> called "the new social order." The major problems of
> this new order were conceived as primarily economic
> in character. But the intellectual climate changed and
> made way for other concerns. There was a new inter-
> est in psychological problems.

It was a group of students supported by Clara Mayer which petitioned Johnson to invite Sandor Ferenczi, a major colleague of Freud, to come from Budapest to give a systematic course in psychoanalysis. Johnson (1952, p. 284) wrote: "The petition came to me as a sort of shock. I had held myself aloof from the psycho-analytic concepts that were floating around liberal New York." But Ferenczi came and taught for many years at the New School. Later, also spurred by student demand, Alfred Adler and Franz Wittels joined the faculty as well.

Other schools of psychological thought were widely represented. John B. Watson taught behaviorist theory. Kurt Koffka
and Gustav Koehler lectured on gestalt psychology. This encour-
agement of teachers from all major schools of thought was one of
Clara Mayer's chief contributions. She later wrote:

> Had there been a department of psychology, with a for-
> mal chairman, such a thorough sampling of the field
> would have been impossible, but at the New School such
> radically different points of view were tolerated as a
> matter of course. The adult world was being offered
> there the most important developments in the whole
> field.

The New School provided a home for other institutions created
to serve adults. Johnson created the University in Exile, a daring
program that brought refugee scholars fleeing fascism to this country as teachers; the École Libre, which attracted exiled French
scholars; and the Institute for World Affairs. A New School graduate faculty developed.

Each of these organizations had its own director. Clara
Mayer headed the School of Philosophy which, with the School of
Political Science, continued to be the undergraduate credit and non-
credit core of the New School.

Johnson, who brought scores of European scholars here to
reestablish their careers, became increasingly involved in international intellectual life, describing his main role as public relations
inside and outside the New School. The New School, a natural home
for exiled scholars, would never have developed without him. But
it was Clara Mayer who initiated these men and women into the
educational life around them, who continued to lead the development
of the curriculum, who made this open university function with a
minimum of administration, and who encouraged and succeeded in
retaining on its undergraduate faculty as distinguished a group of
foreign and American scholars as has ever taught students in an
American institution.

During the 1930s programs in dance, design, and theater
drew faculty of great talent to the school, just as academic fields
had. Erwin Piscator's drama workshop became so important that
the New School ultimately established it as a separate unit. It was
not a technical school, nor was it created for the academic study of
the performing arts. It was a university program designed for the
practical and intellectual development of the arts. There was very
little opportunity for such study in the colleges and universities.
Miss Mayer wrote: "There had been so much teaching about the

arts in academic institutions that it seemed important to give these students a chance to study the visual and performing arts."

Adult education has had little status in this country: we have been wedded to the education of the young. Education for adults at the New School had no tradition to follow or to combat. It was an undeveloped ground.

The academic style of the New School, unconventional by traditional measures, has always drawn criticism from traditional education. A principal one has been the absence of full-time faculty, a teaching design that depends entirely on men and women also engaged elsewhere in their professionals--usually, but not only, in teaching. Clara Mayer considered this design no weakness, but rather one of the principal strengths of the school, since it widened the field from which good teachers could be drawn. She wrote:

> The large majority of faculty members give only one
> course. It is this minimum time involvement that per-
> mits the teacher to consider remuneration as secondary
> to the pleasure of adult teaching. Clearly, his prin-
> cipal livelihood derives from other sources which may
> be as varied as "full-time" teaching elsewhere, business,
> politics, etc. This part-time faculty can also be chosen
> at a uniformly and significantly higher level. The spread
> of education, the enormous demands on the colleges and
> universities, their increasing numbers, obviously re-
> duces the faculty level at even the oldest and wealthiest
> institutions, given the shortage of teachers. Higher
> adult education, on the other hand, with its attractive-
> ness to the teacher and the relatively slight claim of the
> institution on his time, is free to borrow talent without
> restrictions wherever it can be found, even among the
> nationals of other countries, so many of whom find
> themselves, for various reasons, distributed over the
> world.

She pointed out that professionals in a variety of fields, whose services could never have been secured for conventional college classes, took pleasure in teaching students at the New School, sometimes doing so at their own request. For example, Roscoe Pound offered to teach the philosophy of law. Others came to teach in fields outside their professional activities: John Cage, the musician, an amateur mycologist, proposed, and taught, a course in mush-room identification which led to the formation of the Mycological Society of New York.

Clara Mayer's image of the relation of the teacher to the institution was clear:

> It is the creators of knowledge who should be sought in
> the teaching force for higher adult education. Each
> member himself interprets to a volunteer rather than a
> captive audience his own contribution to culture. The
> motive for honesty is clear, along with responsibility,
> vitality, enthusiasm, desire to have the listener under-
> stand. And so the student has the ideal teacher, com-
> bining intellect and character with the excitement of
> following closely the process of discovery.
>   For the teacher, too, it is the ideal teaching
> situation, "the cream of teaching" to use the quotation
> from one of them. . . . The administration of an adult
> school is a third beneficiary, because administration
> becomes so simple.
>   As to the reality: It is easy to exaggerate the
> extent in which the ideal was realized. But it is im-
> possible not to recognize the fact that the ideal was
> achieved now and then, and that the potential sharpened
> everyone's attentiveness and emotional collaboration.
> There _were_ virtually unknown people lecturing with a
> pioneer's persuasiveness who ten years later became
> authorities and nationally famous; there _were_ well-
> known authorities visiting from their traditional
> academies who spoke with the pioneer's persuasive-
> ness in their own field that they were not allowed to
> use back home; there _were_ famous people about whose
> field almost nothing was known and who introduced the
> general public to that field, long before the academies
> could make up their minds about the validity of the field.

Throughout her years there, Clara Mayer was the principal
unifying force in the New School. She implemented and extended
Johnson's brilliant theories about adult education. It was she who
sought the teachers she felt the school should have, interpreted the
school to the people who came to teach, provided the link between
the faculty and the institution, and gave the gifted men and women who
had lived professional lives in entirely different environments abroad
the understanding of education in America and in that institution
which helped bridge the differences between their previous and their
present lives. It was a rare educational achievement.

JACQUELINE GRENNAN AND THE SECULARIZING
OF WEBSTER COLLEGE: "There is no direction
in which we will not look"

Webster College in St. Louis was the first college under the control of the Roman Catholic Church to sever its connection with the Church and become a secular institution. This was in 1967 and it drew wide public attention. It deserved that attention because the context in which an education takes place--large or small college, public or private, secular or religious--is critical. It is not a matter of better or worse, but of how an institution uses, for the education of its students, the assets and liabilities of its environment.

To understand these educational dimensions one must look beyond the drama of the secularization of Webster College and beyond the personal drama of the woman who headed it as a nun and divested herself of her nun's status at the time the college changed its relationship with the Church. For educators these events, while notable in themselves, are important for quite another reason: they were an inevitable consequence of a long educational--not religious--exploration of what the college had been doing, was now doing, and should do. The shift to secular control was a consequence not of loss or change of faith, but of significant educational change. When the General Council of the Sisters of Loretto applied to Cardinal Archbishop Ritter of St. Louis to transfer ownership and operation of the college to a lay board they pointed out both the financial consequences of expanding the college educationally so that 75 percent of its faculty were lay members, and the fact that the college lacked qualified nuns to fill administrative and faculty posts. The reshaping of the curriculum made the reshaping of the governance necessary for educational and financial reasons.

Like many colleges, especially in the South and West, Webster College grew out of a large personal commitment to education. In this case it was the commitment of three young women, physical and intellectual pioneers, who in 1812 founded a log cabin school in the hills of Kentucky for the children of their settlement.

All three were Catholic. They wanted to found not only a school, but a religious order rooted in the American frontier. Declining to go to Europe for novitiate training or to bring teachers to Kentucky to train novices, they created a religious community, the order of the Sisters of Loretto, that in its purposes and structure did belong to the frontier.

Their order grew. Education was the primary task they set themselves. When the frontier moved, they left their cloister and moved farther west too. They lived as they had to live, met all the threats pioneers met, and continued the tasks of their sisterhood and the education of children.

In 1966 Sister Jacqueline Grennan, then president of the college wrote:

> Some frontiers are geographical. Others are social, intellectual, and even spiritual. In 1915 a new generation of Sisters of Loretto addressed themselves to a new task. In 1915 education for women west of the Mississippi was a rare phenomenon, and there was no real Catholic involvement in those few colleges which had opened their doors to the world of women. (p. 6)

At that time the Sisters of Loretto created a new college, first called Loretto College, then renamed Webster College. Fifty years later, Sister Jacqueline requested that the Church transfer ownership and operation of the college to a lay board, and the request was granted. She compared the secularization of Webster with a business firm giving birth to a daughter company when new and compelling needs cannot be met by the original institution. She regarded the secularization of Webster College as a generative act:

> Why is any institution founded? I submit that worthwhile institutions are founded by groups of people coming together in a new way to do something needed by society which other institutions of the society are not prepared to cope with. Thus, the founding of an institution is always a radical move, a somewhat revolutionary move. If the persons involved were thoroughly satisfied with existing institutions, they would see no necessity to found a new one. The new one is almost always conceived to deal with a specific task. It enlists members who become interested in still newer tasks. (p. 4)

It was the vision of new tasks for education that prompted Sister Jacqueline and the people who worked with her to move Webster College to independent control, so that it might perform an intellectual and educational role that could not be performed under the Church.

Jacqueline Grennan's task was intensive, brief, and far-reaching. She did not have the experience of building her institution from the beginning, as Clara Mayer and Lucy Sprague Mitchell had. She came to Webster College in 1959 after teaching in Texas and Missouri, brought there as an assistant by Webster's new president, Sister Franchetta Barberis. She soon became vice president, then

executive vice president. In 1965, when Sister Franchetta resigned
to become coordinator of the Women's Job Corps in Washington, she
became president. Sister Franchetta's own history makes it abun-
dantly clear that the climate of Webster was hardly cloistered during
her presidency, and two years after Sister Jacqueline took office,
control of the college passed to a lay board.

Sister Jacqueline was an educational revolutionary from the
beginning of her life at Webster. She was outspoken in her criticism
of the quality of education many children received in Catholic schools
in that area.

> The size of most of the classes is appalling. There re-
> mains a great number of undegreed teachers who,
> through misguided zeal, are making a negative rather
> than a positive contribution to our schools. A process
> by which graduates of our high schools are lured into
> parochial schoolteaching under the guise of apostolic
> zeal, rather than invited to prepare themselves so that
> they may justly and fruitfully contribute to the forma-
> tion of young minds in the future, must be cut off.
> (p. 146)

Local Catholic universities were making an important contribution; local Catholic high schools were, with difficulty, meeting professional requirements. Both would be increasingly challenged to
provide money as costs spiraled and funds for education in the religious sector became more difficult to find.

The responsibilities of the college for the education of children
was one of Sister Jacqueline's first concerns. The existence of
Catholic schools for children is justified only if their quality is at
least as good as the qualities one respects in non-Catholic institutions. She wrote: "The grace of a vocation cannot make up for conditions which of themselves make the teachers ineffectual" (p. 147).

In 1960 the college was awarded a grant by the Ford Foundation to develop a new teacher training program and to make a
thoroughgoing curriculum study. This was no parochial enterprise.
Discussions within the college were paralleled by discussions with
distinguished educators: scientists, mathematicians, psychologists,
and historians from Harvard, MIT, Chicago, and other places. It
happened that during those years top mathematicians and scientists
were exploring the possibilities for teaching their subjects to elementary school children. They were concerned with making learning significant as a basic intellectual process rather than fostering
the traditional learning of traditional facts and methods. They had
developed their explosive ideas in their sophisticated university

environment and had actually tried them out themselves in certain elementary schools. Their experience affected the thinking at Webster not only about learning in those disciplines but also about learning itself. A mathematics conference brought some of the most distinguished educators working on these problems to the Webster campus: Jerome Wiesner, Jerrold Zacharias, Philip Morrison, and Jerome Bruner. No program for teaching mathematics, science, or anything else emerged from the discussions. What emerged was a realization that these mathematicians and scientists were opening up possibilities for students at whatever age to engage in original, disciplined, intellectual inquiry, unhampered by the laws and restrictions that had governed established procedures for so long. If this possibility was important in the sciences, it was important in education everywhere and important in life. These discussions gave shape to concerns about education that had been brewing at Webster College for some time.

Curriculum research led to changes. The college opened a laboratory school, developed the performing arts, introduced community-oriented studies that led students to work in all parts of the city, and permitted time off for work on special projects.

Lay people on the faculty increased. By the time Webster was secularized there were 24 nuns and 75 lay people on the faculty, half of whom were non-Catholics. It was now clear that the change had as its goal a college that non-Catholics as well as Catholics would want to come to.

As early as 1963 in an address to Webster College students Sister Jacqueline spoke about Christian education in these terms:

. . . grace must be the most important thing of the Christian life--the sharing of the divine life of Christ which we call grace. The kind of preoccupation which sees the Christian life as a series of rules and regulations, a series of prescriptions and proscriptions, is a deadening kind of structure which smothers the force of the grace of life in vitality and action.

In this framework I believe that we have to re-evaluate our whole position about the future role of education and the Christian world. (p. 133)

Two years later, in a talk to the Xavier University forum she said: "I personally do not believe that colleges and universities ought to be owned and operated by religious orders" (p. 164). Her views about education had already received attention in the press. She was quoted as saying that she would no longer join any separate Catholic learned society. To this she responded:

I say this because I think it is so important that I, as a
Catholic, as one of the many Christians, one of the
many people self-consciously possessed of the grace
of life, be involved in the great mainstream of intellectual movements. If there is an American Psychological Association, I can see no reason in the world
for establishing a Catholic Psychological Association,
but I can see every reason in the world for having
Catholics deeply involved in the American Psychological Association. . . . And so, at the same time, I say
that I would like to throw out Catholic textbooks. I
maintain that I want great textbooks written by Catholics. I want those textbooks to be so good that they
could be used at Harvard or Princeton as well as at
Webster College. We must have persons with the vitality of the grace of life who can see history with such
insight that their works are chosen to be used in the
great educational centers of the country; but not
Catholics who write Catholic textbooks with a Catholic
point of view for Catholic schools. (p. 139)

She spoke of the importance of Catholic students attending non-
Catholic institutions: it was important not only for the students but
for the institutions. Only nonsegregation would achieve the values
that could come from the fullest interchange of beliefs, insights,
and knowledge. This even involved the question of clerical dress:
"With this conviction I am begging that the religious congregations
do something about these medieval habits, so that we can again
assume our citizenship, and that we may, in the free and open market, again volunteer to make our investment in the mainstream of
American society" (p. 115).

In 1965 the discussions about curriculum changes at Webster
were at their height. Their focus was the general education requirements, and central to that discussion was, of course, the
theology requirement. Questioning it was no attack on the theology
course as such, although that course came to be the heart of the
controversy that ensued. For those who wanted to design the curriculum to accommodate individual student planning to allow the
widest opportunity for making serious choices, it followed that
there should be no requirements of particular courses for everybody.
That meant that there could be no theology requirement. This was
the point of sharpest conflict with the Church.

The college continued to plan for new ways for new students.
Talk within the institution, with the Sisters of Loretto, and with the
hierarchy was paralleled by continuing discussions with educators

across the country. A year later the issue came to a head. In a talk to faculty and students, Sister Jacqueline (1967a) said:

> It is my personal conviction that the nature of higher education is opposed to juridical control by the Church. The academic freedom which must characterize a college or university would provide continuing embarrassments for the Church if her hierarchy were forced into endorsing or negating the action of the college or university.

The educational task the college had set itself increasingly created problems in its relations with the hierarchy. Basic to the whole issue was the interest in increasing the autonomy of students, the growing commitment to provide them with resources for making responsible choices about the substance and direction of their education.

The questions thus raised about the viability of the current government of the college became sharply focused:

> (1) Should the General Council of a religious congregation . . . be ex-officio the Board of Directors of a subsidiary corporation in which the task has become highly diversified and complex?
>
> (2) Should an institution of higher education necessarily committed to free inquiry and the frontiers of secular as well as theological knowledge be owned by a congregation which has freely subjected itself to hierarchical control?
>
> (3) In the world of Vatican II, with its emphasis on involvement of the laity and on ecumenism, might not a dynamically Catholic institution be "catholic" in its original sense of universal--truly ecumenical rather than self-consciously denominational? (Grennan 1966, pp. 7-8)

The thinking, discussion, and self-examination culminated in a retreat held by the faculty and administration, after which the General Council of the Sisters of Loretto voted to ask canonical permission to transfer the ownership of Webster College to a self-perpetuating Board of Directors. Sister Jacqueline wrote: "Convinced of the power of religious presence as distinct from the power of religious control, we wish to demonstrate to an open and opening world and to ourselves, that the vital force of faith can live and mature in a diverse and dynamic society" (pp. 7-8). Permission was granted, and in 1967 the college passed to secular control.

One can assess only partially the influences responsible for change in an institution. Surely change developed out of the educational discussions; they were an important force that led to the secularization of the college. A change in governance, in turn, freed the college to move wherever the thinking and discussion led. About the change in government the present president of Webster has written: "It was, I think, the beginning of a series of enabling actions which have changed the college fundamentally, kept it in the forefront of genuinely innovative education throughout the intervening years, and given it its present academic health and vitality" (Gerdine 1977).

He pointed out that abolishing the general requirements, one of the first efforts of Sister Jacqueline and her colleagues, gave the college much desired freedom:

> It meant that inter-disciplinary studies began at an early stage; it meant that students were now free to take elective courses at a more advanced level if they were able to do it; it led to the development of the Contract Center within the last four or five years, where individual learning experiences can be arranged, and prior learning assessed; it led to a "program" approach to the individualized Master of Arts degree, which has been so successful in meeting the needs of adult learners of many sorts. (Gerdine 1977)

The conviction that educational change was needed, which led to these new practices, lay behind the move to secularize, and that step led to the rest.

As to Jacqueline Grennan herself, her educational convictions led to a critical change in her professional life which paralleled the change in the college. Even before she became president--indeed almost immediately after she came there as assistant to the president--she became actively engaged in creating educational change. This process brought her in touch with some of the most active and advanced thinking about education in a period seething with controversy. Moreover, both the need for change and the direction of change were central to her thinking about what students should experience: an increasing understanding of and involvement in the critical issues of this time in history, wherever that involvement might lead. What was important for the college and the students was also important for her professional life, and she became increasingly interested in public activities. This interest created problems both for her and for the Church.

At the same time that she communicated to the students and the public the plan to change the governance of the college she wrote to the Archbishop of St. Louis:

> I believe deeply in the work we are doing at Webster College and see my role in it as a personal fulfillment of my Christian commitment. In the last few years I have been aware of the tensions about nuns being involved so fully in the public sector. In some real sense, I share your conviction that nuns, in the commonly accepted image at least, have no business in the public sector. Perhaps in the future, a new form of religious commitment under lay auspices will provide the framework for dedicated women in such roles. However, I am convinced with you that the juridical form of present religious orders is not a viable mode for fulfilling my commitment in the public sector. (1967b)

She also wrote to the Superior General of the order asking for the official application forms for a dispensation from her vows. This dispensation was granted, and it ended Jacqueline Grennan's career as a nun.

She is now president of Hunter College in New York.

LUCY SPRAGUE MITCHELL AND BANK STREET
COLLEGE: "How will we find teachers who will
understand what we are trying to do?"

There is no way to measure the degree to which an educational conviction or way of working owes its success to the temperamental environment in which it is born, the spirit of the conviction that creates it, or the conviction itself. But it is not possible to read the account of the creation of the Bank Street College of Education in New York City without recognizing that it was a temperament as much as anything else that gave it style and character. These qualities have made a strong mark on the teachers, researchers, and students in the school.

From its beginning in 1916 the institution has been developed by people who have worked as colleagues in a common enterprise, and without whose joint endeavor the idea could not have grown into full life. But in discussions about the origin and youth of their enterprise, they leave no doubt that the source of it all was Lucy Sprague Mitchell.

The importance of temperament to the atmosphere and the people of Bank Street is suggested by Lucy Sprague Mitchell's statement in the first catalogue of the teacher education program: "We are interested in imbuing students with an experimental, critical, and ardent approach to their work, and to the social problems of the world in which they, as adults, must take active part. If we accomplish this, we are ready to leave the future to them" (Bank Street College of Education 1931).

Ardor is rarely asked for in college catalogues, but it is a quality that informed everything Mrs. Mitchell did. Its importance to building the institution is evident in the account of how she created that school. The school's history shows that ardor was a catalyst which sparked the creativity of others. Her convictions gave cohesion to the separate activities that developed, and together constituted Bank Street.

She had a good start for developing an interest in education. She graduated with honors in philosophy from Radcliffe College, having studied with Josiah Royce, George Santayana, and Hugo Munsterberg. John Dewey was her friend. She lived with the George Herbert Palmers while she went to college. In 1903, several years out of college, she was invited by the president of the University of California to go there as an assistant professor of literature and the first dean of women. There had been no woman dean at the university, no dean of women, and no women on the faculty; she was looked at askance on all three counts. Some faculty members suggested that she be given the title warden, familiar to the women's colleges in the East, but she managed to avoid that.

She observed that nobody was interested in educating women, particularly for the professions. She began to explore possible fields for women by becoming acquainted with women successful in jobs concerned with human concerns. On leave of absence from the university she spent time in Chicago with Jane Addams at Hull House and with Lillian Wald in New York, where she went with the nurses from the Henry Street Settlement as they did their work on the Lower East Side. She roomed with Florence Kelley, who was working on labor legislation, followed Pauline Goldmark, who was doing social research for the Russell Sage Foundation, and worked at the Salvation Army. She brought back to Berkeley ideas for change in the university curriculum, but what she had mainly learned was that philanthropy could not cure, could not even effectively palliate, social ills.

She spent her last days of leave with Julia Richman, who was attacking the problem of public education through the school system in New York. She wrote on this time of enormous importance for her:

This is the work for me. . . . Public education is the
most constructive attack on social problems, for it deals
with children and what they need to make them grow whole-
somely. It requires experimentation in curriculum for
children and in teacher education. It requires understanding of our culture. It is the synthesis of all my interests,
all my hopes for humanity. I returned to Berkeley with a
clear focus in my own life from which I have never since
deviated. My whole later work life in New York had public education as its aim, but it took over thirty years in
New York before I could get into actual working relations
with the public schools. (Mitchell 1953, p. 210)

Lucy Sprague Mitchell developed working relations with schools
when she founded the Bureau of Educational Experiments in New
York in 1916. Nearly 15 years later a program of cooperation developed in which eight schools worked jointly with the Cooperative
School for Teachers to educate student teachers. These eight
schools were the original cooperating schools and not the New York
City public schools, with which she and the staff were able to begin
working in 1943. Writing later she stated her position:

Our early work with children and teachers required
small schools, fluid situations, where experimental
work could be carried on and full records kept. But
such work we always regarded as preliminary laboratory work. Public schools always held our deepest interest, and our ultimate aim was to make our contribution
to public school education. (1950, p. xxiii)

This activity became the Bank Street College of Education.
Fifteen years of work with children and teachers lay behind
Bank Street College. The design originally evolved from other
activities and ideas, as it has since evolved to include new activities
and ideas, all consistent with its origins. To understand how the
college came about and why it had and still has the character that
marked it from the beginning and that has greatly influenced the
education of teachers, it is worth following Mrs. Mitchell's activities.
In 1913, just married to Wesley Clair Mitchell, she began a
groping effort to discover how to find the work she wanted to do with
children in public schools. She took courses with John Dewey at
Columbia and at Teachers College on public administration and
teaching techniques. She began to attend the public meetings of the
Board of Education, a practice she long followed. Lillian Wald suggested that she start a school for young children at the Henry Street

Settlement, but she felt she knew too little and was doubtful about a school in a settlement house. She worked as a volunteer in the department dealing with mentally retarded children, trained to give psychological tests at the Neurological Institute, and worked with Elizabeth Irwin's experimental public school classes.

She offered her services to the Public Education Assocation, working with Harriot Johnson of the Visiting Teachers, who served as liaisons between the schools and the parents of children in trouble. In Caroline Pratt's Play School, later the City and Country School, she found a way to work with children that was congenial to her interests.

During these years she herself taught children. From her major effort in children's literature came a new way of thinking about books for children. As Blos wrote (1975): "Lucy Sprague Mitchell took seriously the possibility of relating the young child to the real world through the content of literature. She not only freed them from a choice between the fantastic and the humdrum; she also pioneered a new, challenging, and disciplined form of literary expression."

She developed in remarkable detail ways for teachers to help children see, understand, and use their environment in learning. This was a major educational concern. She developed a concept of geography as a means of illuminating relationships between places and between people and places. She became expert at mapmaking and at ways to teach both children and teachers to understand and make maps. Through this imaginative use of cartography she helped children discover and understand their relationships with their families, schoolmates, teachers, and others. For her learning involved being located in one's self and in all the environments of one's life. Her Young Geographers published in 1934 is still requested by teachers.

The late 1920s were a time when people from many disciplines were being called on to use their knowledge for the development of children. Mrs. Mitchell observed that these knowledgeable professionals all worked in terms of their own disciplines and rarely developed working relationships with each other. An organization had to be created to bring together these people whose interests and training were focused on child development. Mrs. Mitchell had the extraordinary luck to be given funds from a private donor to support such an organization for ten years. She lost no time. She provided the Bureau of Educational Experiments with its own nursery school and brought together teachers, psychologists, doctors, anthropologists, and social workers to study children and to pool their findings.

This interdisciplinary approach was conceived by a perceptive person who, though not trained in research, realized that to enhance the growth of children, the insights of people with diverse capacities and knowledge had to be summoned and coordinated. This diversity gave the bureau its character and defined the design by which teachers were to learn their art. It was clear to Mrs. Mitchell that a new way to teach must be found if teachers were to understand children and foster their growth. The Bank Street College of Education was the inevitable outgrowth of the Bureau of Educational Experiments.

But the bureau first had to find its way. The cooperative activity that characterized its life was established. It had no director. Mrs. Mitchell chaired a working council of staff members with major responsibilities. Her task was administrative, and the council reported to a board of trustees. As she wrote: "Suddenly, it seemed, two groups of pioneer workers, the research-minded and the school-minded, focused their interest on children. And the job of the infant Bureau was to get these two groups to make a joint study of children and to have their study profitable to both" (1950, p. 459).

It was a time of struggle. Some of the efforts were clearly directed because some goals and procedures were clear, and others were confused because there were no precedents. In a world in which new psychological ideas and convictions created new controversies daily, where should the college turn for advice? Should John B. Watson, whose conceptions of behavioral psychology were eagerly followed in some quarters, help design the proceedings? Should Robert Woodworth's psychological position guide their thinking? How much was the college to be governed by the research that lay behind the pronouncements about the validity and importance of the IQ, or by the discovery that a child had an unconscious? Franz Boas provided his particular kind of anthropological insights. It was a time of immense intellectual concern with human growth and personality.

The group placed a good deal of trust in careful multiple observations of children: their language, play, and drawings. Those in the organization who taught the children and those who brought their own research interests and skills to the observation of children accumulated new knowledge of the total character and quality of children's lives in school and out.

Everyone was impatient: the growing knowledge about children would not find its most rewarding use until these new insights and ideas moved beyond articles in journals and files in researchers' offices, right into the children's own classrooms. Only teachers could make this happen. The question became How will we find teachers who will understand what we are trying to do? The obvious answer was to create a place to train teachers who shared the bureau's attitudes toward children's growth and the understanding to foster it.

Two years after the bureau was founded a nursery school was established to serve as a laboratory for the teacher education program. The bureau's theories about how children grow and what schools should give them governed the educational character of the School for Teachers.

The School for Teachers was planned without regard for credits, grades, or examinations. It became a successful enterprise before it finally adopted these things in order to obtain from New York State the power to grant degrees and thus certify their students. Recalling the decision 30 years later, Barbara Biber, one of the first people to bring specialized knowledge to the Bureau wrote:

> Growing up seemed the right term for all the years . . .
> each step was a gain, a plunge forward; but something
> had to be left behind, lost, regretted, remembered nos-
> talgically and foregone for the sake of what was gained.
> There was something so pure, so brave, so stirring
> about the experimental teacher education program, free
> of the shackles of points and degrees and licenses and
> certification. . . . But there had to be the day when we
> went to Albany, with our application for a Master's de-
> gree in our arms. . . . With the Master's degree a qual-
> ity of freedom was lost, but without it, our dreams would,
> in these times, have become social vapor, to the lasting
> detriment of many teachers and children. So we grew up
> and lost and gained. (1961)

A substantial spiritual investment goes into creative activity, even (perhaps especially) when it deals with the bureaucracy of a vast governmental institution, in this case the public school system. It was public education in New York City to which the work of this new School for Teachers was ultimately directed. From the time Mrs. Mitchell walked the wards of a public school with Julia Richman and attended meetings of the Board of Education, her aim was to serve the public schools. When the school for teachers was established, she and her associates could have established their own private elementary school. Instead they established a cooperative program with eight interested private schools that were willing to be looked on as experimental, to serve as laboratories for student teachers to study education as it was designed at Bank Street. Students attended these schools four days a week and participated on weekends in seminars, classes, and conferences at Bank Street. Mrs. Mitchell wrote later:

> Why did we try this difficult and complicated setup in-
> stead of establishing a school of our own which would

carry our nursery children up through elementary school
ages? Primarily because we wanted to work with other
neighborhood experimental schools, not to be their rival.
This difficult plan of organization was another example of
our belief that, in the long run, joint thinking of a group
of schools could accomplish more than a single school
could. We felt our student teachers, when they assem-
bled for week-end work at Bank Street would enrich that
work if they brought experiences from schools with a
variety of environments--city, suburban, and rural--with
children of parents with a variety of social and economic
backgrounds . . . with directors and teachers who had
slightly different educational emphases and techniques
though all in agreement on basic attitudes toward children and their education for the modern world. (1953,
p. 470)

Carried over to the design of the school for teachers was the
belief in the importance of direct experience that had been at the
basis of Mrs. Mitchell's work with the children she herself taught
and her writing for children. She had fostered new experiences
with language and the arts, and with field trips and other activities
outside the classroom. If such experiences were important for
children, they were important for the people who were to teach the
children. The weekend arrangement gave the student teachers opportunities to work at Bank Street in laboratories and studios and to
engage in field trips. The student teachers did not first study about
children and later enter the classroom, as was the custom in most
teacher-training programs. They began to work in classrooms at
once; their courses were conducted as seminars using school experience as the basis for their discussions.

The collaboration with the eight schools provided invaluable
knowledge about children and learning. In time, field placements
were expanded to offer students experience in a variety of public
schools, the practice now followed.

In-service workshops were established in the schools, and
Bank Street worked increasingly with teachers who were already
teaching in addition to student teachers. Evening courses for teachers, mainly from public schools and day care centers, now reach
500 students a year. The Bank Street idea has permeated the thinking of teacher education schools all across the country.

After the school began to award master's degrees, the New
York City Board of Education released five teachers from their classrooms and assigned them to work with other teachers as staff members in the Bank Street workshops. The Bank Street staff continued to
work with committees of the Board of Education in an unusual union.

Thirty years after the college published its first catalogue Barbara Biber (1961) gave testimony to the sturdiness of the original idea and the commitment:

> We were a "cause" at first, but we have gone on to see a "cause" mature into a potent professional institution. There could be no other way. Yet, I hope that there will always be something of that quality of a "cause" sustained, if that means a hard core of principles and ideals never to be forsaken or compromised. If those who pick up where we leave off can do this, our memories will have meaning beyond the short stretch of our professional lives.

REFERENCES

Bank Street College of Education. Catalog. New York: Bank Street College, 1931.

Biber, B. Address at a Conference Honoring Eleanor Hogan. Unpublished. June 14, 1961.

Blos, J. Dimensions of Language Experience. New York: Agathon Press, 1975.

Gerdine, L. Letter. February 7, 1977.

Grennan, J. Where I Am Going. New York: McGraw-Hill, 1966.

Grennan, J. Announcement to Faculty and Students. Unpublished. January 11, 1967a.

Grennan, J. Letter to His Eminence, Joseph Cardinal Ritter, Archbishop of St. Louis. January 2, 1967b.

Johnson, A. Pioneer's Progress. New York: Viking Press, 1952.

Mayer, C. Unpublished papers. No Date.

Mitchell, L. S. Our Children and Our Schools. New York: Simon & Schuster, 1950.

Mitchell, L. S. Two Lives. New York: Simon & Schuster, 1953.

New School for Social Research. First Announcement of the School. New York: New School, 1919.

3

Women's Education: the Case for the Single-Sex College
Susan Romer Kaplan

It has long been a woman's problem to choose between the roles of housewife and career woman. The conflict between the roles of wife-mother-professional, between femininity and competence, is a theme that runs steadily through women's educational history. From birth through maturity, society provides girls with cues on how to behave. Although young women are encouraged to excel in certain areas, social pressure also makes them anxious when they are successful in areas not considered feminine.

This conflict of roles reaches its apex during the college years. Mirra Komarovsky, a Barnard College sociologist, has pointed out that girls are told to get good grades, but are also warned about being too smart, a posture that might intimidate men. In interviewing Barnard women, Komarovsky found that two out of five admitted that they play dumb on dates although they are bright and capable students (Chafe 1972).

Matina Horner, president of Radcliffe College, said:

> A bright woman is caught in a double bind. In testing
> and other achievement-oriented situations she worries
> not only about failure, but also about success. If she
> fails, she is not living up to her own standards of per-
> formance; if she succeeds she is not living up to so-
> cietal expectations about the female role. Men in
> our society do not experience this kind of ambiva-
> lence. (Carnegie Commission on Higher Education
> 1973, p. 77)

Role conflict lingers with women even after they have proven themselves professionally competent in a man's world. Arlie Hochschild (1975), an associate professor of sociology at the University of California, Berkeley, who often brought her baby to campus for office hours, described her conflict over being a mother and a professional:

> I also felt envious of the smooth choicelessness of my
> male colleagues who did not bring their children to
> Barrows Hall. . . . I feel it too when I see wives
> drive up to the building in the evening, in the station
> wagon, elbow on the window, two children in the
> back, waiting for a man briskly walking down the
> steps, briefcase in hand. . . . Whenever I see simi-
> lar scenes, something inside rips in half, for I am
> neither and both the brisk-stepping carrier of a brief-
> case and the mother with a packed picnic lunch. The
> university is designed for such men, and their homes
> for such women. It looks easier for them and part of
> me envies them for it. Beneath the envy lies a sense
> of my competitive disadvantage vis-à-vis the men to
> whom I am compared and to whom I compare myself.
> Also beneath it, I am aware of the bizarreness of my
> experiment with the infant box, and paradoxically
> aware too that I am envious of a life I would not really
> like to live. (p. 72)

A woman, unless she chooses not to marry or to marry but
not to bear children, must deal with two conflicting priority systems, career and family. The college experience of a woman may
well determine her choice of one over the other, or it may offer her
the tools to balance both successfully.

Different types of higher education institutions will have different effects on women. Most women are educated in coeducational
institutions, whose impact will differ from that of single-sex colleges. Recently many single-sex institutions have become coeducational: for example, Vassar College admits men and Yale University has opened its doors to undergraduate women. Enough time has
elapsed since these changes to assess their educational and social
impact on women. Some colleges have remained single-sex: Mills,
Wellesley, Mount Holyoke, and Smith Colleges have retained their
historic position and educate only women. There is a certain logic
behind their decisions. Regional cooperation, such as the Twelve
College Exchange in New England the the Bryn Mawr-Haverford College relationship in Pennsylvania, is another approach to defining
the place of women's colleges and their relationships to other institutions.

EARLY HISTORY

Harvard College, the first American institution of higher education, was founded for men in 1636. However, it was not until 1837,

when women were admitted to Oberlin College, that formal higher
education became available to women. Many people were concerned
that women could not stand the strain of such education, either
physiologically or emotionally. Consequently, formal education for
women consisted of seminaries and academies, which were glorified
high schools rather than colleges. In 1821 Emma Willard founded
Troy Seminary. Although mathematics was encouraged over stitch-
ery, the seminary was no more than a preparatory school. Mount
Holyoke Seminary, started in 1836, was also preparatory. Not until
1850 did Mount Holyoke take on the standards of men's colleges. In
1836 the Georgia legislature established Georgia Female College.
In the North, a group of clergymen and laymen decided in 1855 to
open a real college for women, Elmira Female College.

The Civil War was a turning point in the struggle to offer
women an education comparable to that at leading men's institutions.
In 1860 Matthew Vassar gave $400,000 to create a college with a
curriculum modeled after that in men's colleges. Smith was founded
in 1871, Wellesley in 1875, Bryn Mawr in 1880, Radcliffe in 1879,
and Barnard in 1889. Although the women's colleges attempted to
follow the men's model, they found that they had to provide remedial
education as well, since the academic background of the women
varied so much. Several women's colleges had preparatory departments as well as college-level courses until the beginning of the
twentieth century (Feldman 1974).

Graham (1970) has noted that the impetus to educate women
after the Civil War resulted in shrinking college enrollments.
Women's participation in these colleges would help fill empty seats,
and the tuition would help keep the institution financially viable.
Another economic force that helped spur women's education was the
need for school teachers in the West. The Morrill Act of 1862,
which provided for the land-grant colleges, widened educational opportunities for women. The crucial question then became how to
maintain a viable relationship between higher education and domesticity. This conflict between domesticity and competence has been
instrumental in shaping the ideologies and curricula of women's colleges and coeducational institutions throughout their histories.

IMPACT OF WOMEN'S COLLEGES

Women's colleges were founded to provide women with equal
educational opportunities. The need to continue single-sex education
for women today depends in part on whether women at such institutions gain more academic competence and confidence than they would
in a coeducational institution dominated by men. What should

women's education be today and what environment can best provide it? In 1973 Mount Holyoke President David B. Truman said that women's education:

> . . . should confront the destructive stereotypes and
> their symptoms as explicitly as possible; it should
> encourage independence, initiative, autonomy and in-
> volvement; it should encourage the widest possible
> range of opportunities for testing and assessing com-
> petence, and not merely academic competence; and it
> must provide assurance, not indulgence but assurance,
> that the effort to break the stereotypes, to achieve
> real choice, and to compete with anyone of compar-
> able talent is possible as well as desirable, however
> difficult. (Baker 1976, p. 108)

Studies have shown that women's colleges best provide the environment for the development of women's full potential. Tidball (1973) randomly selected 1,500 women from Who's Who of American Women, 1966-1971. The sample represented graduates from women's colleges and coeducational institutions from 1910 to 1960. She found that achievement output, measured by outside success in fields of endeavor, was proportionally twice as great for women's college graduates as for graduates of coeducational institutions. One measure of institution productivity is the percentage of B.A. recipients who earn Ph.D.s (Tidball and Kiskiakowsky 1976). In analyzing data from the National Research Council's Doctorate Record Files from 1920 to 1973, Tidball found that women's colleges are the major contributors of women with Ph.D.s. Male Ph.D.s come from large universities or small, private, coeducational institutions. The analysis demonstrated a clear distinction between the B.A. origins of men and women receiving doctorates. According to Tidball (1974), certain characteristics in a college environment help produce successful women. The most important is the correlation between the number of achievers and the number of women faculty members in the college. She found that "the development of young women of talent into career-successful adults is directly proportional to the number of role models to whom they have access" (p. 52). Another important factor is the need for a large number of women students in an institution to foster women achievers. The greater number of men students, the fewer the women who become achievers. In a male-dominated college, as in the rest of society, women assume a more passive role.

The college years provide time for a woman to review and to reconsider these values and commitments she had adopted through socialization. A young woman can determine during these years the kind of person she wishes to be. Although this period includes great conflict between being accomplished and being female, these are critical years in developing talents. An advantage of educating women separately is that women, worried about their femininity despite their desire for competence, need not be concerned about appearing too bright or studious in an all-female class. Women feel free to speak out in class since they are not competing with men in this environment. They are encouraged to enter so-called male fields such as science and mathematics because professors have only women from which to select. Perhaps most important is the role model found in the preponderance of women faculty on campus (Carnegie 1973). To develop the talent of undergraduate women requires visible women academic professionals. The faculties of women's colleges today, including full- and part-time members, are approximately 50 percent women.

> According to the 1974-75 catalogs, Barnard led the Seven Sisters with 59.1% women on the faculty. Wellesley followed with 55.1% women and was followed in turn by Smith (40.4%), Mount Holyoke (40.3%), Bryn Mawr (40%), and Vassar (39.5%). Radcliffe remains dependent on the Harvard faculty, which remains heavily male. (Baker 1976, p. 7)

Although Tidball's research is important, it has limitations. Is Who's Who of American Women the most reliable source of successful women in this country? Is earning a Ph.D. degree the best means to determine success, or perhaps just one measure? Although it is the women's colleges, particularly the Seven Sisters and Hunter College, that produce a high percentage of doctoral women, these women are already self-selected as achievers before they enter college. Often their social and economic situation allows them the luxury of attending graduate school and provides emotional and financial support. What happens to those women who attend women's colleges and are not labeled successful?

Recently women's colleges have been showing their faith in the leadership ability of women by selecting women to head the institutions, a reversal of the policy of the 1950s and 1960s when the presidents were men. Jill Conway of Smith, Matina Horner of Radcliffe, Rhoda Dorsey of Goucher College, Martha Church of Hood College, and Alice Emerson of Wheaton College in Massachusetts are some of these women presidents.

Of 28 presidents of the Seven Sisters Colleges, since the founding only two have combined career with family: Millicent

McIntosh of Barnard and Horner of Radcliffe. Mary Bunting of Radcliffe and Barbara Newell of Wellesley were both widows while
president (Baker 1976).

COEDUCATIONAL INSTITUTIONS

Throughout the history of higher education the majority of
women have attended coeducational institutions. By the end of the
nineteenth century most public colleges and universities admitted
women. However, it is generally agreed that the purpose of coeducation was not to raise the status of women but to assist the institutions economically. Some colleges also felt that it would be more
natural to have women on campus. Oberlin, the first institution to
admit women, had women students do the domestic chores. Classes
were not held on Mondays when the women were required to do the
laundry and repair the men's clothing. Daily cleaning and cooking
were tailored to class schedules (Conway 1974b).

> There was not in the entire discussion of the Oberlin
> experiment a sustained and serious debate about what
> coeducation might provide for the training of the
> female mind, except an adequate preparation for
> marriage and the capacity to serve as a companion
> for a frontier minister who might otherwise suffer
> from cultural deprivation. Women's minds during
> and after college education were thus considered
> only from the point of view of the services they might
> provide for men. (Conway 1974a)

Have the basic assumptions underlying coeducation today
changed since Oberlin admitted women? Are coeducational colleges and universities places where women may be educated but
where the development of women's academic potential is not a major
goal? Recent findings by David C. McCleland of Harvard, David
Winter of Wesleyan, and Abigail Stewart of Boston University showed
that, by the time they are seniors:

> . . . women at the Ivy institutions have developed a
> much greater "fear of success" than they had when
> they entered college. Men at the same institutions
> lost some of this fear during their undergraduate
> years. The psychologists concluded that a rise in
> the fear of success was "peculiar" to the Ivy campus

whose students finished college "more afraid of competing or standing out" than when they began it.
(Jacobson 1976)

According to Conway, "The decade 1964-1974 has seen a new awareness of the extent to which coeducation at the undergraduate level
has failed to bring women into positions of authority in the definition
and transfer of knowledge" (Conway 1974b).

Coeducational institutions do not provide many women faculty
models. Recent studies of women faculty in general have shown
that, although women represented approximately 46 percent of the
undergraduates and 33 percent of the graduate students, in 1975
they comprised but 21 percent of the professors, an increase of a
mere 2 percent over 1969. The Project on the Status and Education
of Women (1976) found that women as a group today occupy just
about the same status in the university as they did in 1969: "They
spend more time teaching than men; they earn less money than men;
they receive less support for research and publish less than men;
and they show a 'striking pattern of segregation' in regard to rank,
in regard to subjects taught, and type of institutional affiliation"
(p. 4).

Rossi found no women among the 44 full professors in the five
leading sociology departments in the country: Berkeley, Chicago,
Columbia, Harvard, and Michigan. The Committee on the Status of
Women in Economics found that only 6 percent of all economics faculty members in four-year colleges and universities were women
(Carnegie Commission on Higher Education 1973). Leonard (1975)
found that at Harvard there were 20 women and 36 minority-group
men among 766 full professors in 1975. White men still have the
edge in the job market, obtaining high-status jobs through the old-
boy system.

Even in the so-called women's fields the percentage of women
faculty on the academic ladder is small. A report from the University of California, Berkeley (1976) indicated that in 1975 the School
of Education had three women among the 45 ladder-rank positions,
the French department had two out of 11 positions, and sociology
had three out of 23. Despite the agitation of the 1960s, the role of
women in academe has scarcely altered.

Women are rarely found in administration. Less than 5 percent of the colleges and universities in the United States are headed
by women. In 1976 only four public institutions with enrollments
over 10,000 had women presidents, while no private university was
headed by a woman (Project 1976).

According to Mattfeld: "The popular view that academic excellence and prestige of an institution are directly proportional to

the number of men in it and to the prevalence of their values, interests, and concerns in all areas of its endeavors is pervasive in
American higher education" (Mattfeld 1974).

If Tidball is correct about the importance of female role
models to undergraduate women's success, the lack of such models
in a coeducational institution could indirectly affect women's attitudes about women.

SINGLE-SEX INSTITUTIONS THAT HAVE GONE COED

The economic depression in higher education has prompted
many single-sex colleges to go coed. In 1967-68 Vassar, faced with
declining admissions and poor financial prospects, flirted with marriage to Yale and a move to New Haven. At the last moment it with-
drew because it felt that its faculty and students would not be regarded as equal by Yale. The faculty was also concerned about the
extent of Yale's commitment to either undergraduate or women's
education. Instead of merging with Yale, Vassar opened its own
campus to men. In an attempt to alter its ladylike image, the college imported male administrators. A man was appointed to the
new position of vice president for student affairs, and another man
became admissions director. Men were added to the full-time faculty, which was expanded 30 percent to accommodate the hoped-for
increased enrollment. The percentage of full-time women faculty
dropped from 42.9 percent in 1967-68, a year before coeducation,
to 38.2 percent in 1973-74. The percentage of women department
chairpersons dropped from 38 percent to 19 percent in this period.
However, the percentage of women instructors, lecturers, and nonladder appointments increased from 50 percent in 1967-68 to 70 percent in 1973-74 (Baker 1976). Today classes are dominated by men
students, who have also taken over the leadership of student government and publications.

An alumna of Vassar wrote:

> I sensed an underlying attitude of bending over back-
> ward to show how groovy it was for boys at Vassar,
> and how well they were adjusting, and how cute every-
> one thought it all was; accompanied, of course, by the
> playing down of news about girls at Vassar. I began
> to form a nightmare vision of the masculinization of
> Vassar: the president was a man; the older women
> teachers, as they passed into emerita status, were,
> I was sure, being replaced by ambitious young men

who would scorn intimate contact with students in their
rush to get the next scholarly article published; in an
effort to make male students feel comfortable at
Vassar (admittedly an enormous problem), men would
be encouraged and their needs attended to at the expense of the women. I felt a great sense of loss; the
need for sanctuaries for women, far from becoming
obsolete, has become, if anything, more acutely
recognized. (Lydon 1973, p. 81)

Yale, unable to merge with Vassar, opened its doors in fall
1969 to 580 undergraduate women. Pepper Schwartz and Janet
Lever, two (1973) Yale graduate students who interviewed a random
sample of 50 men and 50 women students, found that the women had
great personal doubts about their identity on the Yale campus. A
great majority accepted the premise that their scholarship was different from the scholarship of their male classmates. Some women
thought there was a masculine way of acting in class. Although the
women felt comfortable doing well academically, they did not want
to enter open competition with the men. Women defined themselves
as quietly competent. The men claimed that the top intellects were
men, although some did admit knowing a few of what they called
"super-scientist-type" women. Many men felt it was beneficial to
have women in class because they contributed a feminine viewpoint.
Both men and women mentioned the male monopoly of leadership
positions at Yale. In student government, men tend to be president
and women accept the presumption of male leadership.

When Schwartz and Lever made their study, there were only
43 women faculty members at Yale on a faculty of 839 to act as role
models (Schwartz and Lever 1973). Only two held tenured positions.

Although intelligent women have been admitted to Yale, this in
itself is not recognition by the university that women have the right
to education and to preparation for a lifetime career equal to that
offered men. Different assumptions underlie women's education at
Yale: generally speaking, they are there to provide good companion-
ship and potential wives for future male leaders. Perhaps this is not
so different from the assumptions that underlay the admission of
women to Oberlin in 1837. By 1972 coeds from Yale and Princeton,
concerned about their second-class status, began to return to the
women's colleges.

The underlying assumptions at male-dominated institutions,
coupled with women's early socialization, make it difficult even for
bright, capable women to be assertive. The role conflict between
being feminine (or datable) and being competent cannot help but shape
women's attitudes in the classroom and on the campus. It is difficult

for both men and women to eliminate the social responses of a lifetime. Instead of having four years of college to build confidence in
one's intellect and ability, many women find they are stereotyped by
the established institution before they have had a chance to test
their abilities. Most young women between the ages of 18 and 22
want to be attractive to men. Few dare be more competent than
seems desirable.

MAINTAINING SINGLE-SEX INSTITUTIONS

Despite the financial stresses facing small women's liberal
arts colleges, some have opted to remain single-sex despite the
security that merger with a stronger men's institution might bring.
These colleges recognize a specific mission for women's college
which differs from that of a coeducational institution.

When she was inaugurated as president of Mills College,
Barbara White (1976) emphasized the need for women to reevaluate
their roles and opportunities. She said women have always accepted
society's notion of what they can or cannot do. It is important for
them to rid themselves of stereotypes that hold that the woman is
the nurse, not the doctor, or the woman is good at details so she is
the secretary, not the lawyer. In explaining Mills' choice to remain an undergraduate college for women, White defined the purpose
and mission of a women's college:

The college for women says by its very existence that
a woman should have every opportunity to develop her
potential to the full. It is dedicated wholly to that end;
all its resources, without competition, go to that purpose. All its energies are channeled toward helping
women prepare for meaningful lives, a task far more
difficult for them than for men because of prejudices
that still permeate our society, and because of the
additional obstacles facing women who wish to com-
bine family with careers worthy of their talents. . . .
We are not constructing a lacy ivory tower. We are
preparing women to live as full participants in a complex society in partnership with one another and with
men--with equal responsibilities as well as equal rights.
We are not a college without men, we are a college for women. We are not a protective community;
we are a strengthening and reinforcing community.
(pp. 9-10)

Barbara Newell (1973), president of Wellesley, which has remained single-sex, has held that women's colleges can be leaders
in affirmative action because the women there take on positions of
leadership both as students and faculty. A women's institution, as
a role model for coeducational institutions, must be sensitive to the
particular needs of women. She further indicated that Wellesley was
making arrangements for part-time faculty positions for women with
families so they would not lose their places on the ladder, for shared
jobs, for daycare facilities, and for paternity as well as maternity
leave. As a result of tremendous fund-raising efforts Wellesley had
plans to develop its physical plant during the next ten years. Part
of these plans included a $14 million science complex. Wellesley
was also exploring ways to provide the first two years of medical
education in cooperation with another institution. Wellesley hopes
to offer by example a statement on opportunities for women. Its
environment will help young women better understand women's role
and place in society and free them of the old choice between spinster-
hood and career (Lefkowitz 1970).

REGIONAL COOPERATION

Regional approaches to sharing resources among campuses
allow for exchanges while the colleges maintain their unique historic
character. Many institutions, including Smith, Mount Holyoke,
Amherst, University of Massachusetts, Hampshire College, Bowdoin,
University of Connecticut, Dartmouth, Trinity College, Vassar,
Wellesley, Wesleyan University, Wheaton, and Williams, participate
in cooperative arrangements where students enroll and live on other
campuses for a semester or an academic year.
Bryn Mawr and Haverford have a small regional exchange program. In this case, it was the men's college that turned to the
women's college in time of economic need. Haverford, afflicted
with a $2 million deficit, tried to merge with Bryn Mawr in 1974.
Bryn Mawr wanted to keep its autonomy but was willing to engage in
an exchange. Each campus has maintained its identity, but options
have opened for both. Baker has found that the arrangement has expanded the facilities and enlarged the intellectual community for all
at a minimal expense and a minimal threat to identity (1976).

ROLE OF PUBLIC POLICY

Today the golden years of higher education are over. Gone
are the abundant funds for physical expansion, research grants, and

faculty development. Whether one accepts Cheit's concept of a new depression in higher education (1971) which he replaced with an improved opinion about what he termed "fragile stability" (1973), or the more positive views of Bowen and Minter (1976), there is no doubt about the income-expenditure squeeze in most higher education institutions. This is particularly true of the private sector.

Public policy must determine whether maintaining private institutions, which educate only 23 percent of those enrolled in higher education, is justified. The quality of these institutions can be maintained only if federal and state governments provide more financial aid to them and their students.

What role do these private institutions play that would warrant great outlays of money for their maintenance? Bowen (1968) said:

> The special contributions and problems of the private
> universities must, then, be seen in the light of their
> role as an essential component of a diverse, complex,
> diffuse, and yet highly responsive system of higher edu-
> cation, a system whose value to the nation has been
> amply demonstrated. In this context, private universi-
> ties appear in proper perspective as a precious set of
> "assets-in-being." They help promote freedom, diver-
> sity, and excellence. If their effectiveness is impaired,
> American higher education as a whole will suffer. (p. 62)

To provide the special assets of private education to a wider circle of students, there must be a way to offset high tuition. Both federal and state grants-in-aid directly to students and outright grants to private institutions must be increased to allow low-income students to choose institutions that best fit their needs rather than their pocketbooks.

Many private institutions are liberal arts colleges. In a time of specialization and vocationalism is there any need to maintain liberal arts education, or has it outgrown its usefulness? Mattfeld (1974, p. 287) said: "We must revitalize liberal education only because it remains the best means yet found by which scholars, artists, and teachers can contribute to the solution of the critical conditions that threaten to engulf the human race."

The small liberal arts college can also respond to human needs and aspirations. Bowen (1975) cited a study by C. Robert Pace which describes students at a variety of institutions from 1950 to 1970:

> In virtually every measure, the liberal arts colleges
> outpaced the rest of the field. This was true in in-
> volvement with faculty and peers, satisfaction and

stimulation from the academic program, critical thinking, social awareness, tolerance, individuality, cosmo-
politan outlook, philosophical interest, aesthetic interests, and participation in civic, political, and artistic
activities. The consistency in the many variables reflecting intellectual and personal development was
striking.

The liberal arts college can provide an environment that pro-
motes the emotional and intellectual growth of its students, fostering a sense of community among those who participate in its life.

The factors that support the maintenance of private liberal
arts colleges in general also provide the rationale to maintain separate women's colleges. In the diversity of higher education, one
choice for women should be single-sex education. Studies have
shown that single-sex institutions provide an environment conducive
to women's success. Women's colleges might even serve as models
for coeducational institutions to provide equal opportunity for women.
Women should have the choice of single-sex or coeducational education, depending on their needs and inclinations.

REFERENCES

Baker, L. I'm Radcliffe! Fly Me! New York: Macmillan, 1976.

Bowen, H. "Why Preserve Liberal Arts Colleges?" Change 7,
    no. 6 (1975): 9, 72.

Bowen, H., and Minter, W. J. "Private Higher Education." Second
    Annual Report on Financial and Educational Trends in the Pri-
    vate Sector of American Higher Education. Washington, D.C.:
    Association of American Colleges, 1976.

Bowen, W. G. The Economics of Major Private Universities.
    Berkeley: Carnegie Commission on Higher Education, 1968.

Carnegie Commission on Higher Education. Opportunities for Women
    in Higher Education. New York: McGraw-Hill, 1973.

Chafe, W. H. The American Woman. London: Oxford University
    Press, 1972.

Cheit, E. F. The New Depression in Higher Education. New York:
    McGraw-Hill, 1971.

Cheit, E. F. The New Depression in Higher Education--Two Years Later. Berkeley: Carnegie Commission on Higher Education, 1975.

Conway, J. K. "Coeducation and Women's Studies: Two Approaches to the Question of Women's Place in the Contemporary University." Daedalus 1 (1974b): 239, 249.

Conway, J. K. "Perspectives on the History of Women's Education in the United States." History of Education Quarterly 14 (1974a): 1-12.

Feldman, S. D. Escape from the Doll House. New York: McGraw-Hill, 1974.

Graham, P. A. "Women in Academe." Science 169 (1970): 1284-90.

Hochschild, A. R. "Inside the Clockwork of Male Careers." In Women and the Power to Change, ed. Florence Howe. New York: McGraw-Hill, 1975.

Jacobson, R. L. "It Does, It Doesn't, Matter Where You Go to College." Chronicle of Higher Education 13, no. 10 (1976): 1, 12.

Lefkowitz, M. "Final Report on the Education and Needs of Women." Wellesley, Mass., September 1970. (ED 081 329)*

Leonard, W. J. "Affirmative Action at Harvard." Chronicle of Higher Education 10, no. 6 (1975): 13.

Lydon, S. "The Case against Coeducation, or I Guess Vassar Wasn't So Bad After All." MS 2, no. 3 (1973): 52-53, 81-83.

Mattfeld, J. A. "Liberal Education in Contemporary American Society." Daedalus 1 (1974): 282-87.

Newell, B. "Separate Education for Women." Wellesley Alumnae Magazine (Spring 1973): 1-6.

---

*A number in parentheses, preceded by "ED" refers to an Educational Resources Information Center (ERIC) document.

Project on the Status and Education of Women. On Campus with Women 13 (April 1976).

Rossi, A. "Status of Women in Graduate Departments of Sociology, 1968-1969." The American Sociologist 5, no. 1 (1970): 1-12.

Schwartz, P., and Lever, J. "Women in the Male World of Higher Education." In Academic Women on the Move, ed. A. S. Rossi and A. Calderwood. New York: Russell Sage Foundation, 1973.

Tidball, E. M. "Perspective on Academic Women and Affirmative Action." Educational Record 54 (1973): 130-35.

Tidball, E. M. "The Search for Talented Women." Change 6 (1974): 51-52, 64.

Tidball, E. M., and Kistiakowsky, V. "Baccalaureate Origins of American Scientists and Scholars." Science 193 (1976): 646-52.

University of California, Berkeley. Annual academic personnel report to the Office for Civil Rights. Mimeographed. April 19, 1976.

White, B. "The Inaugural Address of Barbara M. White." Oakland, California: Mills College, 1976.

4

Liberal Arts Education and Women's Development

C. Robert Pace

When one asks a question about liberal arts education today, the response is likely to be an expression of incredulity. What liberal arts education? Is there any? This answer reflects the growth of specialization, the increased interest in career training, and the consequent erosion of former patterns of undergraduate education.

If liberal education is dead, if it has been pushed aside by the demands for specialized training, then why not just give it a decent burial, deliver a brief eulogy, and get on with more important matters? Moreover, in the time span from Plato to the present, whatever benefits liberal education may have had for the affairs of state and the cultivation of taste and virtue were until recently conferred solely on men. How then does one write about women and liberal education? Can one give that topic more than a brief historical footnote marking its arrival and departure?

Contrary to the gloomy prospect implied by these questions, liberal arts education is not prostrate on a sick bed. It may not know clearly where it is going, but it is at least ambulatory. It is possible that women may have as much or more to say than men about its direction and vitality.

CONCEPTS UNDERLYING LIBERAL ARTS

In one sense there is a continuity of meaning about liberal arts education from the Middle Ages to the present. In the Middle Ages liberal education was a disciplined mode of thinking and communicating (the trivium of grammar, rhetoric, and logic) and an exemplary body of content (the quadrivium of music, astronomy, geometry, and arithmetic). Although the language and subject matter may be out of date, the underlying concepts of thought and content still apply to much current rhetoric on the goals and substance of liberal education.

While there is continuity in the idea of liberal education, there has been, of course, a revolutionary change in the content. The liberal education of the trivium and quadrivium was prescientific. Its mode of thought was reason and logic. Science added observation and experiment. As science produced new knowledge and concepts, the content of the liberal arts expanded exponentially. Today this content reflects conceptual advances in the physical and biological sciences and the behavioral and social sciences, as well as the continued relevance accorded to the humanities.

In the college and university curriculum, knowledge is packaged into a vast number of specializations. Nevertheless, for the first half of the twentieth century college students everywhere were likely to encounter a similar pattern of general studies. They took English composition and a foreign language. They often took mathematics and philosophy. There was a science requirement, a social science requirement, and a humanities requirement. Beyond this, students had a major field or specialization and some room for electives. While there were usually many choices in the science, social science, or humanities courses, the pattern or distribution was quite standard and commonly involved somewhat more than one-third of the four-year curriculum.

In the post-World War II years, and more particularly in the past decade, this common pattern has eroded. This change is well documented by a report for the Carnegie Council on Policy Studies in Higher Education (Blackburn 1976) which indicates that the undergraduate curriculum today is divided into three approximately equal components: one-third each general education, major field, and electives. Compared with those of ten years ago, these proportions reflect no change in the time allocated to the major field, a decrease in the time given general education, and an increase in the time for electives. Within the general education component, there has been some decline in the requirement for specific courses. For example in 1967, 90 percent of the institutions required a course in English composition compared to 75 percent today. In 1967, three-fourths of the institutions had a specific foreign language requirement; today about half have such a requirement. Nevertheless, a general or liberal education still comprises one-third of the undergraduate curriculum, still reflects a belief in the relevance of critical thinking and effective communication, and still defines, through distribution requirements, important content as sciences, social sciences, and humanities.

STATEMENTS ON GOALS AND OBJECTIVES

Although liberal arts education may be somewhat harder to find in the curriculum than it used to be, it is not hard to find in statements of goals or objectives. An examination of objectives, however, reveals a new element: an emphasis not only on content, but also on what is supposed to result in personal character and commitment from exposure to that content. This includes responsible citizenship, personal and social maturity, and various attitudes, interests, appreciation, and values.

Typical statements of objectives of general or liberal education are expressions of faith and hope, and they should be read with charity. Below are selected statements included in large-scale research inquiries. Some inquiries have been addressed to students, alumni, faculty members, and administrators asking for judgments about the importance of the objectives. Others have been addressed to students and alumni to measure the extent to which they believe that college contributed to their progress toward or attainment of such objectives.

The first set of objectives comes from a 1949 survey of Syracuse students, faculty, and alumni (Pace and Troyer 1949). The objectives included in the Syracuse questionnaire were brief versions of longer statements included in the report of the President's Commission on Higher Education in 1947. In the alumni version of the questionnaire, former students were asked "How much did your own college experience help you toward attaining these goals?" The goals included writing clearly and effectively; speaking easily and well; developing social competence; understanding other people; discovering personal strengths, weaknesses, abilities, and limitations; understanding world issues and social, political, and economic problems; learning how to participate effectively as a citizen; understanding scientific developments and processes and their applications in society; learning how to think clearly, meet a problem, and follow it through to a solution; developing an understanding and enjoyment of literature, art, and music; understanding the meaning and values of life; and developing a personal philosophy and applying it in daily life.

A nationwide questionnaire survey of upperclassmen and alumni from more than 80 colleges and universities, conducted at the University of California, Los Angeles (Pace 1974) included a checklist of educational benefits. Alumni, for example, were asked to indicate to what extent they benefited in broadened literary acquaintance and appreciation; awareness of different philosophies, cultures, and ways of life; social development or experience and skill in relating to people; personal development or understanding one's abilities and limitations, interests, and standards of behavior; critical thinking, such as logic, inference, nature and limitations of knowledge; esthetic sensitivity, such as appreciation and enjoyment of art, music, and drama; writing and speaking clearly and correctly and communicating effectively; understanding and appreciating science and technology; increased civic awareness, such as understanding and interest in the style and quality of civic and political life; appreciation of individuality and independent thought and action; and tolerance and understanding of other people and their values.

A study of college graduates conducted by the National Opinion Research Center (Spaeth and Greeley 1970) included goal statements that were also part of a questionnaire addressed to faculty members and administrators (Gross and Grambsch 1974). These goal statements included: producing students who have their interests cultivated to the maximum; developing the inner character of students so that they can make sound, correct moral choices; producing good consumers who are elevated culturally, have good taste, and can make good choices; training students in methods of scholarship, scientific research, and creative endeavor; producing well-rounded students whose physical, social, moral, intellectual, and esthetic potentialities have been cultivated; producing students who are able to perform their civic responsibilities effectively; and assisting students to develop objectivity about themselves and their beliefs and to examine those beliefs critically.

A checklist of goal statements for undergraduate education from a survey of faculty members undertaken by the American Council on Education (Bayer 1973) included: conveying a basic appreciation of the liberal arts; increasing the desire and ability to undertake self-directed learning; developing the ability to think clearly; developing creative capacities and moral character; providing for students' emotional development; achieving deeper levels of student self-understanding; and developing responsible citizens.

In 1972 the Educational Testing Service published the Institutional Goals Inventory, which has been widely used in surveys of students, faculty members, administrators, and other groups. The respondent is asked to indicate how important each goal in the inventory is at the institution and how important it should be. Some of the goal statements from the inventory include: helping students identify their personal goals and develop means to achieve them; ensuring that students acquire a basic knowledge in the humanities and social and natural sciences; increasing the desire and ability of students to undertake self-directed learning; helping students achieve deeper levels of self-understanding; ensuring that graduates have achieved some level of reading, writing, and mathematical competence; encouraging students to become conscious of the important moral issues of our time; increasing students' sensitivity to and appreciation of various art forms and artistic expression; helping students understand and respect people from diverse backgrounds and cultures; and training students in scholarly inquiry, scientific research, and problem definition and solution.

These sets of goals and objectives document the similarity in what has been considered important in the objectives of liberal and general education in nationwide surveys. All refer to critical and scientific thinking and include statements about philosophy, ethics, and morality. All refer to responsible citizenship and to the arts or expressive capacities. All include one or more goals related to personal and social development, referring directly or indirectly to such personal qualities as tolerance, appreciation of other cultures, self-directed learning, and so forth. Implicit in all sets and explicit in many is the acquisition of knowledge that includes the sciences, the social and behavioral sciences, and the humanities and arts.

Most of these statements refer not only to knowledge and skills but also to attitudes, values, actions, and commitments. The goals of liberal arts education embody an integration of knowledge, values, and action within the individual. In other words, it is not sufficient to conceptualize liberal education solely as content or curriculum, nor is it adequate to evaluate liberal education programs solely by subject-matter achievement tests.

CONTRIBUTIONS OF COLLEGE
TO GOAL ATTAINMENT

To what extent do students think their college experience contributed to the attainment of these objectives? More particularly, are there important differences in the responses of men and women?

The first evidence comes from the study of 2,000 Syracuse alumni (Wallace 1949) which included graduates of the classes of 1927, 1932, 1937, 1942, and 1947. Reflecting the concept of liberal education as a disciplined mode of thinking and communication, the Syracuse questionnaire listed three objectives: thinking clearly, writing effectively, and speaking effectively. For clear thinking and effective writing, the responses of men and women do not differ. For effective speaking, the proportion of women claiming "much" benefit from their college experience is significantly greater than the proportion of men. Reflecting the concept of liberal education as a body of content worth thinking about, the Syracuse questionnaire listed seven objectives. For the social science objectives of understanding world issues and developing effective citizenship, the replies of men and women do not differ. For science, a substantially higher proportion of men than women attribute "much" influence to their college experience. For the humanities (literature, art and music, and philosophy) the proportion of women

claiming "much" benefit from their college experience is in each
instance substantially greater than the proportion of men. Reflecting the concept of liberal education as the attainment of certain
personal attributes, the survey listed four objectives: social competence, understanding others, self-understanding, and developing
a personal philosophy. For each, the proportion of women attributing "much" influence to their college experience is substantially
higher than the proportion of men.

Additional evidence comes from the UCLA study of alumni.
The more than 8,000 respondents were graduates of the class of
1950 from 74 colleges and universities. The alumni were asked,
"To what extent do you feel you were influenced or benefited in each
of the following respects?" They could respond with "very much,"
"quite a bit," "some," or "very little." For clear thinking and
effective communication, the responses of men and women do not
differ significantly. For objectives related to philosophy and citizenship, the responses also do not differ. However, for literature
and the arts, the scores of women are significantly higher than the
scores of men, and for science, the scores of men are significantly
higher than the scores of women. Reflecting the concept of liberal
education as the acquisition of desirable personal attributes, the
national alumni survey listed four objectives: for self-understanding
and for appreciation of individuality and independence, the responses
do not differ, but for social development and for tolerance and understanding of other people and their values, the scores of women
are significantly higher than the scores of men.

The results from these two alumni surveys, 20 years apart,
are remarkably congruent. For those who may doubt the reliability
and validity of retrospective opinions about progress toward these
objectives, there is additional evidence from the Syracuse and the
national alumni surveys to allay skepticism. In both surveys one
major section of the questionnaire was a series of activity scales or
checklists. The activities included some that were commonplace
and easy and others that required more time and effort and implied
a greater degree of interest and personal or public commitment.
The respondents were asked to check each activity in which they
engaged during the past year. The extent to which people participate
in certain activities presumably reflects their interests, values,
and satisfactions. The relevance of activities to outcome of higher
education is obvious where the activities have some connection with
the content and emphasis of college study. It would be useful to ad-
minister achievement tests in the major fields of knowledge to a
large cross section of college alumni 20 years after graduation.
Since both the psychology and the logistics of this kind of inquiry are
formidable, no one has yet attempted it. To some extent activity

scales can be regarded as an adult-level counterpart of achievement tests, not in the sense of measuring knowledge but of revealing continued interests.

The number of activities checked in each scale provides a reliable score. In the Syracuse study, a second copy of the questionnaire was sent to a sample of the original group which was asked to fill it out again six months later. The median correlation between the scores on the activities scales on those two occasions was .83, and no scale had a test-retest reliability lower than .70. Moreover, 85 percent of the individual item responses were identical on the two occasions. One can be quite confident, therefore, that these reports of activities are reliable.

In the Syracuse survey, there were two activity scales related to social science objectives: politics and civic affairs. The scores of men and women do not differ on either of those scales. Three scales were related to humanities: literature, music, and art. On all three, the mean scores of women are significantly higher than those of men. On the scale related to science, the mean score of men is significantly higher than that of women.

On particular activities, participation differed significantly for men and women. For science activities, for example, men indicated much more often that they discuss new developments in science, read science news, attend lectures or listen to science programs on the radio, visit a science museum, or look up the answer to some science question in a reference volume. For humanities, women indicated much more frequently that they read motion picture, theater, and book reviews, listen to dramatic programs on the radio, attend plays, talk about books with their friends, listen to symphony programs, attend concerts, play a musical instrument, or listen to serious music by contemporary composers. They also talk about art, visit an art gallery or museum, attend an exhibition of contemporary painting, and do art work themselves more frequently than men.

In the national survey, the activities scales were similar in content to those in the earlier Syracuse study; indeed, many items were identical. Among the four activities scales related to the social sciences, the level of participation by women is higher than that by men on the scales for community affairs and intercultural affairs. Responses do not differ on the scales for politics and international affairs. Humanities objectives were represented by four scales: art, music, literature, and drama. On all, the participation level for women is substantially higher than that for men. On the one scale related to science, the participation level for men is substantially higher.

The results of these two surveys are consistent. Judged not only by self-reports of progress toward important objectives but also by subsequent involvement in activities related to those objectives, humanities goals are clearly more fully attained by women than by men. The opposite is true for science goals. Social science goals and the goals of critical thinking and effective communication are attained about equally by men and women. For personal attributes, women ascribe more influence to their college experience than do men.

When reported in percentages, results from the nationwide survey of college graduates add another perspective. The following is the percentage of all graduates who indicated that they were influenced or benefited "very much" or "quite a bit": critical thinking, 72 percent; personal development, 66 percent; awareness of different philosophies, cultures, and ways of life, 64 percent; effective communication, 63 percent; broadened literary acquaintance and appreciation, 62 percent; social development, 61 percent; appreciation of individuality and independence, 61 percent; tolerance and understanding of other people and their values, 56 percent; understanding and appreciation of science and technology, 54 percent; esthetic sensitivity, including appreciation and enjoyment of art, music, and drama, 45 percent; and citizenship, 37 percent.

One could dismiss these results as ancient history, based on responses of individuals who went to college 20 or 30 years ago and whose views do not reflect those of more recent generations. However, the national surveys conducted at UCLA in 1969 yielded similar questionnaire data from over 7,000 upperclassmen in 80 colleges and universities. The same list of educational benefits was included in questionnaires for both the upperclassmen and the alumni. Upperclassmen were asked, "To what extent do you feel you have made progress or been benefited in each of the following respects?" The percentages of upperclassmen indicating "very much" or "quite a bit" of progress are identical to the percentages of alumni for the objectives of critical thinking and citizenship. For the objectives of philosophy and literature, the differences between present and former students are slight (not more than 5 percent). For the arts, upperclassmen reported greater benefit (53 percent) than alumni (45 percent). For science, upperclassmen reported less benefit (43 percent) than alumni (54 percent). The objective "writing and speaking--clear, correct, effective communication," is the only one on which there is a major difference in progress between present and former students. Unfortunately for those who think this goal highly important, only 49 percent of present students reported substantial progress toward its attainment, compared with

63 percent of the alumni. Upperclassmen and alumni differ most on statements describing personal attributes: self-understanding, social development, tolerance, and individuality and independence. In every instance the proportion of upperclassmen reporting major progress is substantially greater than that reported by the alumni.

When differences between men and women upperclassmen were compared, the pattern was nearly identical to that of the alumni sample: no sex differences for critical thinking or effective communication; more women than men reporting progress toward the humanities objectives of literature, philosophy, and the arts; more men than women reporting progress toward understanding science and technology and toward the citizenship objective; and more women than men reporting progress on three of the four objectives related to personal attributes.

It is apparent that these sex differences among both alumni and upperclassmen parallel differences in curricula. More women than men major in the humanities and arts, more men than women major in the sciences, and roughly equal numbers major in the social sciences. Presumably men and women are about equally exposed to professors' expectations for critical thinking and effective communication.

EFFECTS OF PROFESSIONAL SCHOOLS ON GOAL ATTAINMENT

Today, especially in the comprehensive universities and state colleges, there are more students majoring in programs whose purposes are explicitly directed toward vocational and career development than there are in the colleges of arts and sciences. In some cases students can enroll in vocational and professional schools as freshmen; in others, they shift from arts and sciences to the professional schools after one or two years. Most of their college experience is in the context of a vocational emphasis: agriculture, business, education, engineering, fine arts, home economics, journalism, nursing, pharmacy, or social work. What happens to liberal education benefits in this context? An old answer to this question comes from the Syracuse survey of alumni in 1949 (Wallace), and a newer one from the UCLA survey of upperclassmen in 1969 (McCaslin 1974).

An assessment of the relationship between the scores of Syracuse alumni on their participation in politics, civic affairs, literature, music, art, and science and the undergraduate college or professional school in which the alumni had been enrolled was made separately for men and women. With the mean score of all

women on each of the six activity scales considered baseline, one
can note whether the mean score of all women enrolled in one of the
professional schools is higher or lower than this baseline. Those
findings can be compared with similar findings for women enrolled
in the college of liberal arts, majoring in science, social sciences,
or humanities. There were three professional schools: home economics, fine arts, and business administration. Three schools
times six scales equals 18 possible observations of scores above or
below the baseline. The scores of the professional school alumni
are above the baseline in three instances and below in 15. The
same comparison for the three major fields within the college of
liberal arts indicated that scores are above the baseline in 11 instances and below in seven. The data for men revealed the same
clear difference. There were four professional schools: applied
science, business administration, fine arts, and forestry. In the
24 possible observations, the scores of men from the professional
schools are above the average for all men in eight cases and below
the average in 16 cases. Men who had been in the college of liberal
arts are above the baseline in 12 cases and below in six.

If one thinks of adult participation in civic and cultural affairs
as a residual influence of liberal education, this influence is much
more evident among graduates of the college of liberal arts than
among graduates of the professional schools.

A special analysis of the UCLA survey of upperclassmen
yielded a generally congruent conclusion. McCaslin, comparing
the responses of students from ten universities and ten liberal arts
colleges on their estimated progress toward various objectives,
found several differences. Students in the more homogeneous environments of liberal arts colleges reported more progress toward
liberal education goals (specifically those related to philosophy,
literature, arts, personal development, and social development)
than did students in the more heterogeneous environments of large
universities. Only on the science objective is the progress of university students greater than that of liberal arts college students.
Of course the university students included many in vocational programs, as well as those in the college of arts and sciences. When
the university students were divided and liberal arts college students
compared with university students in the college of arts and sciences,
the overall differences were reduced, although there are still significant differences in literature and the arts.

The problem with liberal education in the universities is the
relative lack of it in undergraduate vocational and professional programs. This lack is mainly apparent with respect to humanistic objectives: the proportions of students in the survey expressing major
progress toward "broadened literary acquaintance and appreciation"

are 71 percent in the liberal arts colleges, 62 percent in university
liberal education programs, and 48 percent in university vocational
programs. The proportions of survey students expressing major
progress toward "awareness of different philosophies, cultures,
and ways of life" are 78 percent in the liberal arts colleges, 73
percent in the university liberal education programs, and 64 percent in university vocational programs. For "aesthetic sensitivity
--appreciation of art, music, and drama," the proportions are 61
percent, 55 percent, and 46 percent, respectively. This same
downward progression is also evident for "appreciation of individuality and independence of thought and action" and "tolerance and
understanding of other people and their values."

FUTURE INFLUENCE OF WOMEN

How can women shape the future direction and substance of
liberal arts education? As more women enter the sciences, perhaps the liberal benefits of science can be more fully promoted.
It is astonishing, given the significance of science and technology
for modern society, that the objective of understanding science and
technology ranks close to the bottom of the list of goals toward
which recent students and alumni believe they have made major
progress. As more women enter vocational and career development
programs, their departure from liberal education major fields may
further reduce the benefits that can be attributed to liberal studies.
If past is prologue, one can predict that as enrollment in undergraduate vocational programs increases, liberal education benefits
will decrease. Women have benefited from liberal education to a
greater extent than men, judging by their own estimates of benefit,
their subsequent involvement in civic and cultural affairs, and
their personal and social development. How much value do they
attach to all this? Perhaps at some future time, instead of writing
about liberal arts and women's development, one will be able to
write about women and the development of liberal arts.

REFERENCES

Bayer, A. E. Teaching Faculty in Academe: 1972-1973. Washington, D.C.: American Council on Education, 1973.

Blackburn, R. T. Changing Practices in Undergraduate Education.
Berkeley: Carnegie Council on Policy Studies in Higher Education, 1976.

Gross, E., and Grambsch, P. V. Changes in University Organization, 1964-1971. New York: McGraw-Hill, 1974.

McCaslin, B. "A Comparison of Students' Progress on Liberal
Education Objectives in Universities and Liberal Arts Colleges."
M.A. dissertation, University of California, Los Angeles, 1974.

Pace, C. R., and Troyer, M. E. "Self-Survey: Report to the
Faculty." Syracuse University, 1949.

Pace, C. R. The Demise of Diversity: A Comparative Profile of
Eight Types of Institutions. Berkeley: Carnegie Commission on
Higher Education, 1974.

Spaeth, J. L., and Greeley, A. M. Recent Alumni and Higher Education. New York: McGraw-Hill, 1970.

Wallace, D. G. "A Description and Interpretation of the Activities
and Opinions of Syracuse University Graduates Related to General Education." Ph.D. dissertation, Syracuse University, 1949.

5
Women's Studies: Its Origin, Organization, and Prospects
Sheila Tobias

Women's studies is the intellectual examination of the absence of women from history; a fresh look in a non-Freudian way at the social psychology of women; the study of women in literature and the images of women in the arts; the economic and legal history of the family; and speculation about "androgyny," a state of society and a state of mind where sex differences might be socially, economically, and politically overcome.

ORIGIN OF WOMEN'S STUDIES

Student dissent in American colleges and universities during the late 1960s focused on three issues: university complicity in the Vietnamese war and the defense-related research associated with it; the constitutional issue of university governance, particularly the role of the student as consumer and client; and curricular reform. Although the first two issues received much national and international publicity, the third was also an essential element in the dissident students' rationale for trying to wrest control of the university from those determining the content and structure of higher education. As early as 1965, the Students for a Democratic Society and other ad hoc student and faculty campus activists were establishing free universities and free university courses, intending with these to create parallel and competing educational offerings with as legitimate a claim to college credit as anything else the university offered.

Sometimes the free university course was nothing more than a means to organize politically around a local or national issue, but most often the courses were explicitly designed to fill gaps in the formal curriculum, with titles like U.S. Foreign Policy Since World War II, Marxist Economics, The Cuban Revolution, China, Vietnam,

Black History, and Black Literature. Eventually some of these courses were absorbed into the regular curriculum and others won the funding and academic support necessary to be permanently integrated into programs or, in the case of environmental studies, established as departments. But the crucial issue, whether the university faculty may exercise a monopoly over the structure and definition of knowledge, was not resolved in favor of student demands. Few free universities and free university courses remain today. Only to a limited extent has the student's right to a more relevant curriculum been conceded.

The women's movement came on the heels of these other curricular and noncurricular events. As a result women's studies, sometimes known as female studies, feminist studies, gender studies, or by Kenneth Boulding (1976) as "dimorphics," is to some extent derivative of the ideas and purposes of the free university. Women's studies means courses on women in America and elsewhere, on sex roles, on sex inequality, and on the politics of gender assignment and beliefs about male-female differences. Such courses began without substantial prior organization at many colleges and universities in 1969. Although the impulse toward women's studies was similar to that which stimulated black and ethnic studies, the spread of women's studies and its impact on research and teaching seems to have been far greater and longer lasting.

From the beginning, as Florence Howe (1974), an early proponent of women's studies, put it, the women's movement was a "teaching movement," stimulated in large part by the recognition among women faculty and students that respectable scholarship, quite as much as popular culture, omits, distorts, and trivializes women as a class (Stimpson 1973). It was Kate Millett who called modern social science a religion and male social scientists as comprising a kind of priesthood determining and promoting beliefs about what is appropriate and normal for women and men to think, do, and be (Millett 1970).

By the mid-1960s, feminists had already begun the research that would provide material for women's studies courses. The Feminine Mystique (Friedan 1964) developed a new sociology of women and pointed to the problems of the suburban housewife. Millett's (1970) analysis of patriarchy challenged assumptions about sex differences (psychology), the rationale for a male-dominated culture (anthropology and sociology), and the almost universal preference for male writers and their writing among academics (literary criticism). Alice Rossi (1967), analyzing the low incidence of women scientists and engineers, formed some hypotheses about sex-role socialization. She described a hybrid model of male-female integration (androgyny), which anticipated an adjustment of men's lives to women's needs as well as vice versa. Bem and Bem (1970) characterized the American educational system as one that trains a woman to know her place. Naomi Weisstein (1969) was unforgiving in her exposé of antifeminist biases among professional psychologists in their so-called value-free research and therapy.

In sum, the absence of information about women in the curriculum and the universities' insensitivity to issues of sexual bias and inequality began in the late 1960s to be perceived by women students and faculty as a political phenomenon, rather than as a result of past omissions or a simple failure of academic imagination. The curriculum, reflecting the exclusion of women from power in society, in university administration, and on university faculties, contributed to the collective female sense of being outside the mainstream of human culture (Gornick 1970). With 40 percent of the college-age population attending colleges and universities and thousands of faculty members enjoying opportunities to mold student opinion, the university appeared to women's liberationists as an institution well worth reshaping. Moreover, hundreds of female Ph.D.s, their higher education the direct result of the expansion of American graduate schools after the Sputnik challenge of the mid-1950s, found themselves trained but not sought after as professionals. Their perceived job discrimination at the hands of putatively liberal university men made them angry and radicalized them. Women's studies as a way of examining and eradicating the publicly acceptable prejudice against women seemed a natural next step for academic feminists.

DEFINING WOMEN'S STUDIES

In the late 1960s academic women saw the woman problem, like the Negro problem of yesteryear, as outside the mainstream of American life and thought. It was the reversal of this perspective, together with an aggressive insistence that sex differences be considered as learned until proven otherwise, which characterized the first wave of women's studies courses in 1969-70. It was agreed that so much about women had been excluded or misrepresented that woman herself was an appropriate theme for study. Typical early courses such as Evolution of Female Personality, or Social Roles of Women in America, represented quite simply a desire to know and to teach more about women. Such courses tended to include the history of women, perspectives on contemporary women, a typology of women (artists, mothers, blacks, Chicanos, old women), marriage and child rearing in a cross-cultural perspective, images of women as portrayed in literature, the arts, and popular culture, and, toward the end of the semester, a discussion about alternatives for women (and men) in an androgynous society, defined as one that would minimize, instead of emphasize, sex differences.

Between 1971 and 1976, as women's studies proliferated, course content became more critical of existing academic matter and more broadly based. The progression was not orderly, but was characterized by discoveries of the links between female behavior and the environments in which it is shaped. Those insights and the syllabi generated by them might be summarized as follows:

- Study of Woman: What is a female personality?
- Masculinity and Femininity: What are the implications of these terms? How are they defined? How is the behavior learned? Is it universally the same?
- Female Culture: What is common to the female experience? How would it be evaluated in a non-male–dominated society? Is achievement motivated by a need for affiliation, for example, any less real than achievement motivated by a need for dominance?
- Academic Disciplines: Having discovered the absence of women from history and the minimizing of the subject of sex-role socialization, students and teachers proceeded to examine the disciplines themselves for bias. In this period, feminist literary criticism and fundamental critiques of social science methodology began to appear.
- Male Society and Culture: What are the strengths and weaknesses of the majority when viewed as male instead of human?
- Theory and Practice of Gender: What is the outcome when gender, regarded as a social system for allocating tasks, rewards, and characteristics, is supported by a belief system justifying those arrangements? What are the ramifications of gender as sexism?

Thus in practice, courses in women's studies consider not only what societal roles women traditionally fill, but also what cultural assumptions and economic arrangements account for their secondary occupational status and absence from national leadership. Typically, after an examination of adult roles, the socialization process of women is considered: how the self-esteem of girls is diminished as they learn about sex-role differentiation, how institutions and roles are defined to prove that men and women naturally behave in opposing and mutually exclusive ways. After analysis comes feminist criticism expressed as a belief that prevailing cultural assumptions are particularly damaging to women and frustrating to normal human needs for an expressive life. Thus, both pedagogically and intellectually, women's studies develops into a frank critique of social expectations and economic realities.

Despite this, the majority of women's studies courses is currently taught in the liberal arts by faculty in the humanities, sociology, psychology, and history. Although many subjects should be part of the behavioral sciences, early childhood development, family sociology, industrial relations, organizational theory and behavior, and labor economics, faculty members in these departments have been slower to organize courses on women.

The development of women's studies has not been controlled by a single coherent theory of women's studies or feminist education, although some of the prime movers have written provocatively on the subject. Howe (1970) described women's studies as having two goals: consciousness-raising and compensation. Gerda Lerner (1970) called on women's historians to seek the history of women. Stimpson (1973) argued that women's studies should correct what she termed "omissions, distortions, and trivialization" of women in the traditional curriculum.

In the absence of theory and of carefully delineated goals or objectives, women's studies planning committees in such diverse institutions as Columbia, Cornell, Portland State and San Diego State Universities, and the State University of New York (SUNY) at Buffalo began to bog down in protracted and enervating debates about what women's studies should be and who should be taught and how. As courses evolved into programs or major fields, these issues were confounded by increasing pressure on women's studies to serve the needs of all women within a particular academic community. Suddenly women's studies was expected to provide continuing education, counseling, and job placement in addition to academic courses. Those who believed that women's studies should primarily provide a feminist critique of the disciplines debated those who believed that it should primarily provide a consciousness-raising experience. At SUNY at Buffalo during those years, the Women's Studies College voted to exclude male professors and students from its program, and the university had to threaten legal action to get the committee to open its courses to men.

A considerable number of women's studies programs has had to confront the ramifications of these differing goals. Street women's studies, infusion, and dimorphics are several additional models for the future. But in the period of growth and development between 1970 and 1977, a number of lasting contributions were made. Almost every research journal in the social sciences, the humanities, and law devoted space to women. Five new journals concerned with scholarship about women and gender roles have been established: Feminist Studies, Women's Studies, Signs: A Journal of Women in Culture and Society, Psychology of Women Quarterly, and Sex Roles: A Journal of Research. Research centers on women's issues have been established at Stanford University, Barnard, Wellesley, Eagleton Institute at Rutgers, and the Urban Institute.

Vast quantities of material for teaching, including articles, monographs, and anthologies, are available now in every discipline and cross-discipline. The publishing cooperative, Arno Press-New York Times, for example, in 1973 reissued 200 books relevant to women's history, as well as the official history of women's suffrage. Books by forgotten women authors such as the nineteenth-century writer Kate Chopin are in paperback editions today. Black women writers are important in this rediscovery process: Anne Moody's Coming of Age in Mississippi, originally published in 1968, and Zora Neale Hurston's Dust Tracks on a Road, originally published in 1934, have been reissued. Maya Angelou, Toni Morrison, Nicki Giovanni, and Toni Cade are on many reading lists. All in all, the publishing industry has been responsive to women's studies, undoubtedly because it is both an academic and a marketable subject.

Perhaps the most important intellectual contributions have come in the academic disciplines that impinge on women's studies. Academic women began to discover when they investigated the treatment of women in their own fields that where women do not behave as expected in experiments to test psychological and sociological hypotheses, the female subjects are considered to have skewed the data and are rejected. The hypotheses subsequently drawn about human behavior, however, survive (Horner 1969). In sociology and in home economics, a large subject area in land-grant colleges and universities, a particular, rigid, and highly ethnocentric view of the so-called normal family is presented and justified as corresponding to universal psychological needs. Meanwhile in the humanities, where by far most academic women are located because of sex-typing in their earlier education, women artists and writers are often misunderstood or neglected in the curriculum since, in general, they are undervalued by both male and female readers because of a literary tradition Ellmann (1968) has called "phallic criticism." Ellmann has argued, as so many other critics, that male authors whose vision of the world might be considered narrowly and even adolescently masculine or macho from a woman's point of view are being presented to students as spokespersons for the human condition.

Kaufman and Richardson illustrated the kind of critique and reconstruction in which feminist academics are engaged: In a prospectus for a book, they wrote:

Most social scientists conceive of achievement as an absolute value, seldom questioning its historical and socio-cultural relativity. . . . Little attention, if any,

is paid to political and structural barriers which may
prevent, condition, or even change achievement motivation and behavior. Researchers who look to personal motive alone, without describing the social context within which it is expressed, may be led to the
ultimate fallacy of "blaming the victim" . . . . Certainly personal dispositions contribute to successful
achievement, but we question any conceptualization of
the "need to achieve" that does not encompass the
social and cultural context within which achievement
is measured and defined; and even more importantly,
we doubt that such "need" becomes a stable personality trait immutable or unchanging throughout the life
cycle. (pp. 2-3)

Another critique and reconstruction, this time of the historical
tradition, emerges from consideration of women's history by Joan
Kelly Gadol (1976). Gadol has drawn out the "theoretical significance of women's history and its implications for historical study
in general":

In seeking to add women to the fund of historical knowledge, women's history has revitalized theory, for it has
shaken the conceptual foundations of historical study. It
has done this by making problematical three of the basic
concerns of historical thought: (1) periodization, (2) the
categories of social analysis, and (3) theories of social
change. (p. 809)

With the founding in 1975-76 of Signs, edited by academic feminists and published by the University of Chicago Press, women's
studies came of age in terms of academic status. Women's studies
has won, if grudgingly, the respect and credibility that any new field
or new configuration of research and teaching must win for itself.
At the same time, in the face of budget crises and widespread retreat from curricular experimentation that mark the current academic mood, the outlook for funded women's studies is mixed.
With the exception of the Ford Foundation, which had spent more
than $1 million by 1977 in support of research, evaluation, and co-
ordination, foundations have been indifferent to women's studies.
Thus the future of women's studies still depends on the vitality of
the women's movement and on interest among students. The
strategies for survival taken by those who organize women's studies locally and regionally acknowledge this fact.

ORGANIZATION OF WOMEN'S STUDIES

Without the women's movement, there would have been no women's studies courses or research. The movement gave women faculty members the courage to press reluctant departments and administrators for the release time and the financial support to start new courses. The movement made women students profoundly interested in and supportive of women faculty, and it provided the ideas and research agenda as well. Coming on the heels of black studies and the crisis of relevance in the university, women's studies was able to employ a language and rationale that were already familiar in other contexts.

There is no way to know with certainty the present number of courses and programs. Florence Howe reported at the founding convention of the National Women's Studies Association in 1977 that there might be as many as 4,000 courses. In terms of sheer activity, women's studies has been a powerful academic innovation. Female Studies, an encyclopedia of women's course syllabi and commentary, had 11 volumes by 1977. The Clearing House for Women's Studies at SUNY at Old Westbury publishes Who's Who and Where in Women's Studies and a women's studies newsletter. The national association, which was founded relatively late in the development of women's studies, was explicitly designed to increase the visibility of courses and programs, to contribute toward funding, to protect women in jeopardy because of their feminist activities, and to unite the many groups within the academic movement.

In the beginning there was no organization at all. There were so many women graduate students, instructors, and junior faculty at American colleges and universities assigned to teaching introductory humanities and freshman seminars that it was relatively easy to modify the syllabi of existing courses to incorporate material on women, sex roles, sex differences, and the women's movement itself. Thus, in the early years between 1969 and 1972, and even today where they are new, women's studies courses tended to appear full blown without formal administrative approval. Hundreds of courses on women, ranging from noncredit experimental seminars in prestigious institutions such as Harvard and Yale Universities to large lecture courses at public colleges and universities, have taken hold since 1970. These might have gone unnoticed outside the confines of each campus except that, in an unusual act of sharing and mutual stimulation, faculty members made available to one another their syllabi, bibliographies, and reports on their experiences in teaching women's studies. Discussion among college professors about curriculum, course content, or pedagogy is rare in this country, and the publication of course syllabi was virtually unknown prior to the Female Studies volumes.

The syllabi, together with some regional conferences among women's studies' faculty, spread the idea and the legitimacy of the enterprise more rapidly than would otherwise have been the case. By 1971 student activism was already waning and the universities were about to enter a more cautious and self-protective phase. The New Guide to Current Female Studies (1971) listed 610 courses at 200 institutions employing 500 instructors--163 courses in English, 52 in sociology, 84 in history, and the rest in other disciplines. Since this volume appeared only two years after the first women's studies courses, it represents a remarkable proliferation in a short time.

The first women's studies courses were usually seminars or small colloquia held in dormitories as part of an ongoing introductory course in the humanities or social sciences. Often they were taught by students, nonladder faculty, or nonacademic staff. Only where there was a regular faculty member interested in sponsoring such a course could women's studies appear officially in a college catalogue. Thus the organization of the courses and programs was from the outset a series of pragmatic responses to possibilities that varied from campus to campus.

Unlike black studies, where black faculty had to be recruited, female students could usually find an underpaid but willing female faculty member. At Cornell University a female assistant professor, sponsored by a male full professor, took formal responsibility in spring 1970 for a large lecture course, Evolution of Female Personality, on behalf of a team of teachers who were for the most part regular faculty members.

Where a professor was well established, of course, the subject matter could be added in a new course or integrated into an old one. For example Alice Rossi, when she was at Goucher College, made sex equality a unit in a course on the sociology of equality. Annette Baxter of Barnard College and Gerda Lerner at Sarah Lawrence College both expanded courses on women's history. A home economics department chairman at the University of Kansas and another at the University of Wisconsin at Stout offered new courses on women as part of the traditional human development curriculum.

Where there was no faculty member willing to teach or to underwrite a course on women, students might initiate a program. At Bryn Mawr College, for example, students sat in in fall 1970 to pressure the administration to hire Kate Millett to teach a one-semester course. At Columbia University, students met for a full year in 1971-72 to design a comprehensive program on women's studies before presenting a demand to the administration. During negotiations for a women's studies program at San Diego State University a nationwide write-in campaign was organized on behalf of the pro-women's studies caucus, and at SUNY at Buffalo, where women's studies was launched simultaneously in the College of Arts and Sciences and the College of Social Work, massive student support made the difference. But the initiation and early support for women's studies usually came from women faculty and staff.

Programs varied in structure. At San Diego State in 1970, a proposal was written for a joint large-scale campus-community program. The director, who would be independent of the university tenure system, was to be hired in consultation with students, teachers, and community women. At Cornell University in 1971, a modest budget was requested for a coordinating office that would employ only visiting lecturers and borrow faculty from cooperative departments. At the University of Pittsburgh in 1972, five faculty positions were authorized by the administration as joint appointments in English, psychology, and women's studies, although few of these were actually made. The director was to be an academic woman who would help recruit, hire, and expand the program. At the Universities of Connecticut and Wisconsin in 1975, interdisciplinary programs were headed by a women's studies specialist on the tenure track in an appropriate department.

Of the full-fledged programs in women's studies, few provide a degree although many offer a major. Sarah Lawrence has offered an M.A. program in women's history since 1972. George Washington University has provided an interdisciplinary M.A. with courses in research on women, feminist counseling, or women's studies administration since 1974. Goddard College has an undergraduate major and an M.A. in women's studies.

Experience has shown that it is much more difficult to alter a traditional academic organization in a particular institution to make way for women's studies than to select a structural configuration much like another program already in existence. At Cornell, the model for a time was a Latin American studies program, for no other reason than that it was cross-disciplinary (indeed cross-college) and had no independent faculty. Later, when the dean of a college within the Cornell system announced his willingness to sponsor women's studies, the configuration was redesigned into an intra-college model, but in neither case was an entirely new credit structure created. The black studies parallel is again instructive: much of the difficulty in establishing black studies at most institutions and in giving it credibility and autonomy has resulted from the newness and uniqueness of the structures created to house the programs.

Just as arrangements have varied depending on precedent, budget, and personal preference of students and staff, so too the problems besetting the courses and programs have differed. At Cornell, San Diego State, Pittsburgh, and probably elsewhere, disagreements developed between the academic staff, sensitive to professional criteria for advancement, and the nonacademic staff, anxious to keep women's studies out of the ivory tower. Divisions appeared as early as 1972: street women's studies was assumed to be incompatible with classroom women's studies. Disagreements also developed over the choice of material and the mode of instruction appropriate to courses on women. From one point of view the subject matter could be radical, but teaching techniques and expectations should be traditional. From another point of view, a radical new subject should be experimental in every respect. For some, a final examination in women's studies is absurd. For others, consciousness-raising belongs outside the classroom.

Other controversial issues include the desirability of having men teachers or students in women's studies classes, the degree of specialization for women's studies, the wisdom of graduate programs, and the long-term relation of academic women's studies to the women's movement. These issues become even more urgent as women's studies courses and programs proliferate and mature.

TODAY AND BEYOND

Now that female consciousness has been raised overall, there is increasing pressure on women's studies courses and programs to serve the disparate needs of all women inside and outside the academic community. As a result, a typical women's studies planning committee may deal with a welter of conflicting goals and different constituencies. New issues may emerge: is women's studies supposed to meet the continuing educational needs of adult women, however these are defined? At the University of Minnesota, women's studies is housed in continuing education. If this is to be the rule, how is the field to compete with English and physics for academic prestige? Or, if women's studies is to provide a feminist perspective on the traditional curriculum, should not the subject matter be integrated into regular undergraduate and graduate courses, rather than established as a separate program? Or, if courses in women's studies are to be used to pressure the institution to hire more (or more radical) women for the faculty, what should be the relationship of the professional women already on campus to the program? Their primary goal is to achieve eminence in their own fields; they may feel or feign indifference to women's studies. All these issues are legitimate in an educational institution where half or more of the students are women. The challenge for women's studies advocates is to keep these concerns separable and to set clear priorities among them. Otherwise one runs the risk of having a vice president suggest,

as one did at California State University at Fresno, that a women's
studies course could be replaced with a remedial math course and
expanded women's physical education facilities.

Most academic feminists believe that women's studies can
achieve all three goals: legitimizing the study of women's culture,
continuing the study of man and his world, and providing feminist
education. But the wise women's studies planner will acknowledge
that it may require different programs to accomplish these different
goals in any one institution, given different faculty and constituents.
One program, for example, may properly have both men and women
students; another may not. One may appropriately be evaluated
along standard educational lines; another might be destroyed by such
an approach. One may be enhanced by the participation of male
faculty; another might be undermined by the presence of male authority figures.

The National Women's Studies Association, composed of learners and practitioners of women's studies and committed to feminist
education, yet open to men teachers and students, marks constructive response to these issues. The founding of the association was
tantamount to a commitment to a vision of women's studies which
has room for both academic and community-based activities. The
current decline in youthful college students and the increase in adult
learners could mean that women's studies may be even more important in tomorrow's college curriculum than in today's. Lifelong
learning, with its attention to the returning woman student, guaran-
tees continued interest in women's studies by new students.

Among women's studies goals are the maintenance and expansion of college women's studies, integration of these studies into the
curriculum, the development of street women's studies outside the
classroom, the expansion of women's studies into high schools,
YWCAs, and other learning establishments for young girls, and the
continued critique of the academic disciplines.

OTHER WOMEN'S STUDIES MODELS

Integration of women's studies into the curriculum has been a
risky long-term goal of academic feminism. Unless an institution
commits itself to intensive faculty retraining, like Alverno College,
integration may mean no more than an occasional curricular bow in
the form of a unit on women's suffrage in a history course, on sex
equality in a sociology course, or on sex-role socialization in a
psychology course. Isolating women's subjects in units is not the
best way to integrate women's studies, but it is the most obvious
and the path that traditional faculty members are likely to choose.

Lois Banner (1977), in a preliminary report on the integration of women's subjects into the curriculum, has suggested that this form of integration is more widespread than previously assumed.

Far more effective is reexamining the curriculum and eliminating biases about women and traditional views of gender assignment. Unless this is done, the unit on women may remain marginal to the central themes of the course and will surely be eliminated at some later date by units on more topical subjects. The superficial integration of women's studies does have one advantage, however: more students than could or would be accommodated in specialized women's studies courses and programs will be exposed to a feminist perspective on history, government, economics, sociology, psychology, anthropology, literature, and even medicine and law.

One way to better integrate women's studies is to reperiodize in such a way that a section of a course subject will be taught where the issue of women or sex roles is particularly important. In the history course Men and Women in Wartime, taught at Wesleyan University in fall 1974 and 1975, for example, there would have been no way to eliminate the subjects related to women without radically altering the course.

Outside the classroom but sometimes still within the university, growing out of self-help clinics, workshops, women's centers, newspaper enterprises, cooperatives, and collectives, are vital women's studies courses and programs with different goals and styles of operation. The goals of street women's studies are more behavioral than academic: "to teach women how to achieve freedom, survival, and the satisfaction of their basic needs" (Tobias 1975). The style of operation is collective, noncredit, and generally non-traditional. Feminism is not the first movement to go outside conventional educational institutions to develop a curriculum that combines learning with self-actualization and political action. Nineteenth-century British industrial workers were trained in evening institutes; twentieth-century labor union shop stewards are sent to union-run schools. To the extent that street women's studies meets the needs of community organizers, women about to reenter the labor force, women on welfare, high school students, and alienated housewives, it may well one day exceed classroom women's studies in numbers of programs and students.

In some regions of the country street women's studies and classroom women's studies have been in conflict, largely because their proponents found themselves in competition for limited funds and, in some cases, both sought credits from the academic institution. In some places, as a result of this conflict, street women's studies has moved off campus.

Somewhere between the classroom and the street is still another kind of women's institution. Sagaris, a 1975 summer program
in Lyndonville, Vermont, attempted to meet the needs of women community organizers by bringing them together with academic feminists.
Sagaris included skills-development workshops, leadership-training
sessions, and advanced lectures on poetry, all meant to coexist.
One of the most impressive aspects of Sagaris was the demonstrated
willingness of relatively poor and poorly paid women to raise the
several hundred dollars required to attend. In the future similar
way stations, moving from one campus to another, may well provide
the open and independent structure in which women's studies thrives.

Dimorphics, or the science of two forms, is more than just a
clever way to characterize the study of gender (Boulding 1976). It
points to an epistemological phenomenon that women's studies has
underscored: the tendency among western cultures to perceive certain human differences, notably sex differences, as opposite, dichot-
omous, and nonoverlapping. Under the umbrella of dimorphics,
researchers in women's studies can move beyond the subject of
women per se, or even of men, to the issue of gender as it is regarded in society. Such a redefinition of women's studies would
have one immediate benefit: it would eliminate once and for all the
criticism that the study of gender is marginal to the mainstream of
the curriculum, and is local or ethnic. However, such a redefinition
might also remove the field entirely from the women's movement
that nourished it.

These issues and the new social deterministic theories of behavior emerging from social biology will doubtless be high on the
agenda of the women's studies learners and practitioners who are
organized now to further women's studies.

REFERENCES

Banner, L. "Report on a Pilot Survey of Women in the Liberal Arts
    Curriculum." Report at the National Women's Studies Associa-
    tion meeting, January 1977, in San Francisco.

Bem, S., and Bem, D. Training a Woman to Know Her Place.
    Pittsburgh: KNOW, 1970.

Boulding, K. "The Social Institutions of Occupational Segregation:
    Comment I." Signs: Journal of Women in Culture and
    Society 1 (1976): 75-77.

Ellman, M. Thinking about Women. New York: Harcourt, Brace, and World, 1968.

Friedan, B. The Feminine Mystique. New York: Dell, 1964.

Gadol, J. "The Social Relations of the Sexes: Methodological Implications of Women's History." Signs: Journal of Women in Culture and Society 1 (1976): 809.

Gornick, V. "Woman as Outsider." In Woman in a Sexist Society, ed. V. Gornick and B. Moran. New York: Basic Books, 1970.

Horner, M. "Women's Fear of Success." Psychology Today 3 (1969): 36.

Howe, F., and Ahlum, C. "Women's Studies and Social Change." In Academic Women on the Move, ed. A. Rossi and A. Calderwood. New York: Russell Sage Foundation, 1974, 393-423.

Kaufman, D., and Richardson, B. "Women's Public and Private Roles: Achievement through the Life Cycle." Prospectus for a book, 1976.

Lerner, G. "Women's History." Paper read at the American Historical Association meeting in Boston, Massachusetts, December 1970.

Millett, K. Sexual Politics. Garden City, N.Y.: Doubleday, 1970.

New Guide to Current Female Studies. Pittsburgh: KNOW, 1971.

Rossi, A. "An Immodest Proposal." In Woman in America, ed. R. Lifton. Boston: Beacon Hill, 1967.

Stimpson, C. "The New Feminism and Women's Studies." Change 5 (1973): 43-48.

Tobias, S. Personal interview with members of Sagaris program, Lyndonville, Vermont, summer 1975.

Weisstein, N. Psychology Reconstructs the Female. Pittsburgh: KNOW, 1969.

6

The Undergraduate Woman
Alexander W. Astin

The sheer volume of published research on college students suggests that a great deal may be known about the personal and educational development of undergraduate women. This extensive body of knowledge, however, has not yet yielded a comprehensive picture of the college woman. Many large-scale studies have focused primarily on men (Solmon and Taubman 1973), while others have combined men and women in the same analyses (Astin and Panos 1969; Chickering 1969). The few studies that have focused on women are either out of date or involve only a few unrepresentative institutions, such as Bennington and Vassar Colleges.

A comprehensive profile of the undergraduate woman should include her characteristics at the time of college entry, changes during the undergraduate years, and recent trends in her values, attitudes, and career aspirations. The profile here is based on data from the national Cooperative Institutional Research Program or CIRP, sponsored jointly by the American Council on Education and the University of California, at Los Angeles, an ongoing longitudinal study of the impact of different college environments on student development. The profile shows women's characteristics at the time of college entry and changes during the undergraduate years in four major areas: attitudes, values, and self-concept; patterns of behavior; competence and achievement; and career development. Findings concerning the impact of different college environments on women's development are from a recent study by Astin (1977b).

ATTITUDES, VALUES, AND SELF-CONCEPT

The annual CIRP surveys of entering freshmen contain several dozen attitudinal items on social and national issues. Table 6.1 shows those items where endorsement by men and women differed

TABLE 6.1

Differences in Attitudes of Freshman Women and Men on Social and National Issues, 1976

Attitude	Percent Agreeing Strongly or Somewhat		Difference
	Women	Men	
Capital punishment should be abolished	63	53	+10
Women should receive the same salary and opportunities for advancement as men in comparable fields	96	88	+ 8
The federal government should do more to discourage energy consumption	83	77	+ 6
The federal government should help college students with more grants instead of loans	84	78	+ 6
Scientists should publish their findings regardless of the possible consequences	58	64	− 6
Marijuana should be legalized	46	52	− 6
Realistically, an individual can do little to bring about change in our society	41	48	− 7
Large political campaign contributions from wealthy individuals should be abolished	54	61	− 7
Divorce laws should be liberalized	47	55	− 8
People should be discouraged from having large families	50	60	−10
People should not obey laws which violate their personal values	43	54	−11
Women should be subject to the draft*	16	27	−11
There is too much concern in the courts for the rights of criminals	54	65	−11
The chief benefit of a college education is that it increases one's earning power	49	62	−13
A couple should live together for some time before deciding to get married	43	54	−11
It is important to have laws prohibiting homosexual relationships	39	55	−16
The activities of married women are best confined to the home and family	20	37	−17
If two people really like each other, it's all right for them to have sex even if they've known each other for only a very short time	33	65	−32

*From 1970 freshman survey.

Source: A. W. Astin, M. R. King, and G. T. Richardson, The American Freshman: National Norms for Fall 1975. Los Angeles: Graduate School of Education, University of California, Los Angeles, 1976.

by more than five percentage points in the 1976 survey of entering freshmen. By far the largest difference (32 percent) occurs on the statement supporting sexual relations between recent acquaintances: twice as many freshmen men as women find sex acceptable under these conditions. Men are also more likely to support the idea of living together before marriage, although the margin is somewhat smaller (11 percent difference). This relatively conservative attitude of women toward heterosexual relations is reversed for homosexual relationships: men are substantially more likely (16 percent difference) to advocate laws prohibiting homosexual relationships. Apparently women find homosexual relationships less threatening or distasteful than men, in spite of their more conservative attitude toward heterosexual relationships.

Women tend to take a less punitive and more humane view toward criminals: they are more opposed than men to capital punishment (10 percent difference) and less likely to feel that courts offer too much protection to criminals (11 percent difference). Men, by contrast, take a more libertine approach toward such matters as liberalization of marijuana, divorce laws, and not obeying laws that run counter to one's own values. Women are more supportive than men of job equality for the sexes (8 percent difference) and less supportive of the traditional view that the proper place for married women is with the home and family (17 percent difference).

Responses to these latter two items have shown dramatic changes since the late 1960s (Figure 6.1). In 1967 a clear majority of entering freshmen agreed with the statement: "The activities of married women are best confined to the home and family." Male endorsement (67 percent) was substantially stronger than female endorsement in 1967 (44 percent). Each year since then (the question was not asked in 1968), endorsement by both sexes has declined steadily to the point where, in 1976, less than 30 percent of the freshmen agreed. The steepest declines occurred between 1967 and 1973, at a time when the women's movement was getting into full gear. Since then, endorsement by women has leveled off at slightly less than 20 percent, and endorsement by men has continued to decline to 37 percent.

A similar liberalization of student attitudes has occurred in response to the statement "women should receive the same salary and opportunities for advancement as men in comparable positions" (Table 6.1). Since 1970 (the first year the item was used in the survey), student agreement has increased from 81 percent to 92 percent. Increases have been comparable among men (from 76 percent to 88 percent) and women (from 87 percent to 96 percent). Little change, however, has occurred since 1972, which suggests that roughly 12 percent of the men and 4 percent of the women are hard core sexists when it comes to job equality for women.

FIGURE 6.1

Changes in Student Endorsement of the Statement,
"The Activities of Married Women are Best
Confined to the Home and Family," 1967-76

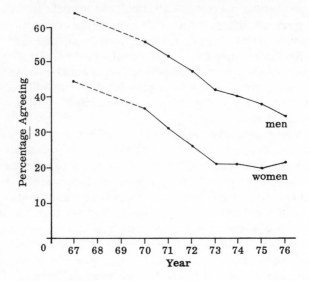

Source: Compiled by the author.

How do the attitudes of women change once they enter college?
Longitudinal follow-ups four years after college entry show that
students of both sexes tend to become more supportive of liberal
views on social issues. On the matter of job equality for women and
rejection of the traditional women's role, women show somewhat
greater changes than men, so the sexes are somewhat farther apart
on these issues after college. Attending a university rather than
two- and four-year colleges and attending an institution located in
the northeastern states is associated with greater than average declines in support for a traditional role for women.

Values

The annual freshman surveys for CIRP contain a number of
statements about students' values or life goals. Students are asked
whether the goal represented by the statement is essential, very
important, somewhat important, or not important. Table 6.2 sum-
marizes the responses of the 1976 freshmen to these items and also
shows changes over the ten years between 1966 and 1976. Items have

TABLE 6.2

Changes in Life Goals of Freshman Women and Men, 1976

Life Goal	Percentage Endorsing "Essential" or "Very Important"		Change 1966-76	
	Women	Men	Women	Men
Business Interest				
Being successful in a business of my own	35	54	- 7	-10
Being very well off financially	45	61	+17	+11
Becoming an expert in finance and commerce[a]	10	22	+ 4	+ 1
Status Need				
Having administrative responsibilities for the work of others	29	35	+16	+10
Obtaining recognition from my colleagues for contributions to my special field	42	49	+ 6	+ 1
Becoming an authority in my field	67	74	+ 6	+4
Athletic Interest				
Becoming an outstanding athlete	4	18	n.a.[b]	n.a.
Altruism and Social Concern				
Joining the Peace Corps or Vista	21	11	- 7	- 2
Developing a meaningful philosophy of life	64	58	-24	-21
Helping others who are in difficulty	72	55	- 7	- 4
Influencing social values	32	28	- 5	- 3
Participating in a community action program	32	26	b	b
Becoming involved in programs to clean up the environment	26	29	b	b
Artistic Interest				
Creating artistic work (painting, sculpture, decorating)	18	11	b	b
Writing original works (poems, novels, short stories)	14	11	b	b
Becoming accomplished in one of the performing arts (acting, dancing)	13	10	b	b
Marriage and Family				
Raising a family	57	58	-21	- 9
Marriage while in college[c]	7	4	- 2	- 3
Marry within a year after finishing college[c]	18	14	-11	- 5

[a]Percentages from 1972 survey.
[b]Not available.
[c]Included in a list of self-predictions. Responses indicate chances are either "very good" or "good."

Source: Compiled by the author.

been grouped into six general categories: business interest, status need, athletic interest, altruism and social concern, artistic interest, and marriage and family. Women express much stronger altruism and social concern than men at the time of college entry. The only exception is the item on programs to clean up the environment, where men show slightly stronger interest. Women also show somewhat stronger artistic interest and interest in getting married. Women have substantially weaker interest in athletics, status, and business.

While these findings confirm many stereotypic sex differences reported in other studies, the data in the last two columns of Table 6.2 suggest that these differences have diminished somewhat for the most recent classes of entering freshmen. For example, while both sexes have shown an increasing interest in administrative responsibility during recent years, the increase among women has been substantially larger (16 percent) than that among men (10 percent). The gap between the sexes has also closed for most other items in Table 6.2. Thus, while stereotypic sex differences still exist among today's college freshmen, these differences appear to be diminishing. Like changes in students' attitudes toward women's roles (Figure 6.2), these trends probably reflect the effects of the women's movement.

FIGURE 6.2

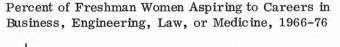

Percent of Freshman Women Aspiring to Careers in Business, Engineering, Law, or Medicine, 1966-76

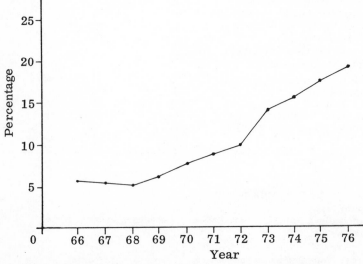

Source: Compiled by the author.

Self-Concept

Freshman self-ratings on a number of personal traits are shown in Table 6.3. On the one hand, women are more likely than men to see themselves as empathic and cheerful, traits commonly associated with femininity. On the other hand, they are less likely than men to rate themselves high in popularity and in specialized skills: mathematics, mechanics, and athletics. This pattern suggests strongly that freshman women have somewhat less self-esteem than freshman men.

TABLE 6.3

Differences in Self-Ratings of Freshman Women and Men on Personal Traits, 1976

Trait	Percent Rating "Above Average"		
	Women	Men	Difference
Understanding of others	72	61	+11
Cheerfulness	61	50	+11
Writing ability	35	31	+ 4
Political liberalism	16	21	− 5
Political conservatism	9	15	− 6
Self-confidence (social)	33	39	− 6
Physical attractiveness	24	31	− 7
Leadership ability	39	47	− 8
Popularity	27	35	− 8
Popularity with the opposite sex	25	35	−10
Self-confidence (intellectual)	37	48	−11
Mathematical ability	27	40	−13
Athletic ability	26	52	−26
Mechanical ability	10	37	−27

Source: Compiled by the author.

Men rate themselves higher on political liberalism and political conservatism. These results are consistent with a separate political self-identification item included in the 1976 freshman survey. On this five-category item, more men (30 percent) than women (27 percent) rated themselves as either liberal or left, and more men (19 percent) than women (14 percent) also rated themselves as either conservative or far-right. Women outnumbered men among middle-of-the-road persons (61 percent versus 52 percent). Clearly, freshman men are more inclined to take extreme political positions than freshman women.

Changes During College

Longitudinal follow-ups four years after college entry show that women change in a number of ways during college, although differences between women and men tend to persist. Thus, women's stronger altruistic and artistic interests are maintained, as are their weaker business and athletic interests and lower interpersonal and intellectual self-esteem. Both women and men show declines in status needs during college, but the declines are greater for women so the gap actually widens with time. The only trait where sexes converge after college entry is political liberalism: although both women and men increase substantially in liberalism after college entry, men increase more, so the relative positions of the sexes are reversed. In other words, women begin college slightly more liberal than men, but men are slightly more liberal four years later. This reversal may be attributed in part to men's greater involvement in campus political activity (Astin, Astin, Bayer, and Bisconti 1975).

PATTERNS OF BEHAVIOR

Freshmen entering college between 1966 and 1971 were asked how frequently they engaged in certain behavior during the year prior to college entry. (These behavioral items were discontinued after 1971 to make the freshman questionnaire more suitable for older students.) Many of their responses showed substantial differences between women and men in frequency of some behavior. These behavioral items are grouped into nine general categories (Table 6.4). Women consistently show greater studiousness, religiousness, artistic interest, cooperation and helpfulness, and concern with health. They are less inclined than men to be verbally aggressive, competitive, irresponsible and hedonistic. These categories, of course, are not entirely independent. Studiousness and religiousness, for example, tend to be negatively associated with hedonism and irresponsibility. In fact, the items listed under irresponsibility could just as well be negative indicators of studiousness. Again, these differences reinforce stereotypic sex differences.

TABLE 6.4

Differences in Behavior of Freshman Women and Men, 1971

Behavior	Percent Reporting "Frequently" or "Occasionally"		
	Women	Men	Difference
Studiousness			
Checked out a book or journal from the school library*	60	41	+19
Typed a homework assignment*	33	19	+14
Studied in the library*	36	27	+ 9
Did extra (unassigned) reading for a course*	17	12	+ 5
Religiousness			
Prayed	62	35	+27
Attended church	69	54	+15
Said grace before meals	44	30	+14
Attended Sunday school	59	53	+ 6
Artistic Interest			
Read poetry not connected with a course	76	46	+30
Attended a concert	73	53	+20
Visited an art gallery or museum	63	47	+16
Listened to folk music	41	26	+15
Attended a ballet	21	8	+13
Sang in a choir or glee club	44	32	+12
Wrote a short story or poem	43	31	+12
Wrote an article for the school paper	30	20	+10
Had a part in a play	37	27	+10
Played a musical instrument	37	30	+ 7
Concern With Health			
Used a dietary formula	28	6	+22
Wore glasses or contact lenses	58	47	+11
Took vitamins	64	55	+ 9
Missed school because of illness*	5	2	+ 3
Took a tranquilizing pill	8	5	+ 3
Took sleeping pills	5	4	+ 1
Cooperation-Helpfulness			
Participated in an informal group sing	68	50	+18
Tutored another student	47	40	+ 7
Verbal Aggressiveness			
Made wisecracks in class	49	68	−19
Cursed or swore*	13	29	−16
Argued with a teacher in class	43	55	−12
Called a teacher by his/her first name	20	32	−12
Argued with other students	10	14	− 4
Hedonism			
Drank beer	41	64	−23
Smoked cigarettes*	14	21	− 7
Competitiveness			
Gambled with cards or dice	21	52	−31
Played chess	23	52	−29
Cribbed on an examination	17	25	− 8
Irresponsibility			
Failed to complete a homework assignment on time	60	72	−12
Turned in a paper or theme late	41	52	−11
Overslept and missed a class or appointment	17	24	− 7
Came late to class	51	54	− 3

*"Frequently" only.

Source: Compiled by the author.

Although these items have not been used since 1971, consecutive
freshman classes between 1966 and 1971 showed little systematic
change in frequency of this behavior.

Longitudinal follow-ups showed that many behavioral differences between women and men persist during college. Thus, even
though both sexes show increased hedonism and decreased religiousness in college, women retain their relatively religious and non-
hedonistic position. Women continue to be less verbally aggressive
than men in college, although these more passive tendencies are
more likely to persist in a coeducational college than in a women's
college. This effect of the women's college raises some provocative
questions: given the stereotypic sex roles of male dominance and
female submissiveness, does the presence of men in the classroom
inhibit women from asserting themselves? Are women more likely
to be verbally aggressive in an all-female class?

Attending a college for women substantially decreases the
women's chances of becoming involved in athletics, whereas the reverse occurs for men, who are more likely to participate in athletics
at an all-male college. These contrasting effects could be traced
to the dramatically different environments. An earlier study (Astin
1968) has shown, for example, that women's and men's colleges
differ most in terms of a bipolar factor he labeled "cooperativeness
versus competitiveness." Given the freshman sex differences reported in Table 6.4, this difference in college environments is not
surprising.

A behavioral outcome of considerable significance for women
is marriage. Women are substantially more likely to get married
during college than men, even after their initially stronger marriage
plans are taken into account. While research (Bayer 1969) has suggested that women will be less likely to marry if they attend a
women's rather than a coeducational college, more recent longitudinal follow-ups have indicated that the type of college has little, if
any, impact on women's chances of marrying. The previously reported effect of women's colleges may have appeared because
women entering those institutions are less interested in early marriage than women entering coeducational institutions. When initial
marriage plans are controlled, differences in marriage rates between students in women's and coeducational institutions disappear.

COMPETENCE AND ACHIEVEMENT

Research has consistently shown that women get higher grades
than men both in high school and in college. Table 6.5 compares
the high school grades of men and women entering college in fall 1976.

Women with grades of B+ or higher outnumber men by nearly three to two, whereas men with grades below B- outnumber women by nearly two to one. The last two columns of Table 6.5 show the change in grade distributions for men and women during the past ten years. Both sexes have shown a substantial decrease in lower grades and a corresponding increase in higher grades. This grade inflation seems to be somewhat greater for men than for women. These increasing grades have apparently affected the students' expectation for academic performance in college: during recent years the percentage of women who say they have a very good chance of earning at least a B average in college has increased from 25 percent to 41 percent; the corresponding increase for men has been from 22 percent to 40 percent. Similarly, the percentage of women who expect to graduate with honors has increased from 3 percent to 10 percent; the increase for men has been from 4 percent to 12 percent. Fewer women expect to graduate with honors, in spite of their superior academic performance both in high school and in college.

TABLE 6.5

Changes in High School Grades and Educational Aspirations
of Freshman Women and Men, 1976
(percent)

	Women	Men	Change Since 1966 Women	Men
Average High School Grade				
A or A+	10	7	+ 4	+ 3
A-	14	9	+ 3	+ 3
B+	24	18	+ 4	+ 6
B	28	26	+ 3	+ 7
B-	11	16	- 3	0
C+	9	15	- 4	- 6
C	5	10	- 4	-10
D	0	1	0	0
Highest Degree Planned				
Less than Master's	47	52	-10	0
Master's	29	28	- 1	- 2
Ph.D. or Ed.D.	8	10	+ 3	- 3
M.D., D.D.S.	6	8	+ 4	+ 1
LL.B., J.D.	4	6	+ 4	+ 4

Source: Compiled by the author.

This discrepancy between actual performance and aspirations is reflected in women's degree plans (Table 6.5). Only 18 percent of the women entering college in fall 1966, compared with 24 percent of the men, aspired to Ph.D.s or high level professional degrees such as law and medicine. The gap in aspirations between women and men, however, has been closing rapidly in recent years. Since 1966, the percentage of women aspiring to Ph.D.s or high level professional degrees has increased only slightly. Whereas women accounted for only one in five of the entering freshmen who aspired to such degrees, today they account for better than two in five. These changes in degree plans are further reflected in changes in women's career aspirations.

The educational and intellectual development of the typical college woman differs somewhat from that of the typical college man. Although women earn higher grades than men, they are less likely to complete the degree and to enroll in graduate or professional school. Women's higher dropout rates are attributable in part to their greater tendency to marry during the undergraduate years. Moreover, women's aspirations for higher degrees decline slightly after college entry, while men's aspirations increase during the undergraduate years. Compared with men, women are more likely to acquire general cultural knowledge and skills in foreign languages, music, typing, and homemaking. Men are more likely to achieve in athletics, to publish original writing, to acquire technical or scientific skills, to improve their knowledge of sports, and to improve their skill in swimming and general physical fitness. Some evidence suggests that these sex differences in the development of competencies arise in part from the curriculum: women tend to take a somewhat different distribution of undergraduate courses than men, and these differences generally conform to the differences in skill development.

The pattern of intellectual and educational development for the typical undergraduate woman varies somewhat if she attends a women's rather than a coeducational college. Although women are more likely to achieve in athletics at a coeducational institution, they are more likely to attain positions of leadership, to complete the degree, to aspire to higher degrees, and to enter graduate or professional school if they attend a women's college.

Findings about attainment of leadership positions provide material for speculation on sex roles. While a woman's chances of gaining a student office are somewhat better at a women's college than at a coeducational institution, a man's chances are substantially better at a coeducational college. Women seem to fare somewhat better in the competition for leadership positions if they are not competing with men. Could it be that women are less likely to be aggressive when they are competing with men? Such an interpretation is supported by the finding that women are less likely to be verbally aggressive in the classroom when they attend coeducational institutions. In short, the presence of men students acts as a brake on women's tendency to compete, a finding that supports Horner's (1968) thesis that women experience a fear of success when they compete with men. Although it could be argued that the men's greater success in competing for leadership positions at coeducational institutions may be explained in the same way--that is, men will compete more aggressively if they are in the presence of women--this explanation is not supported by the results for verbal aggressiveness. Men are not less likely to be verbally aggressive in men's colleges than in coeducational institutions. Sex bias may also be a consideration: persons who elect student leaders may tend to favor men over women, independent of past accomplishments or qualifications.

CAREER DEVELOPMENT

The most popular career choices among women entering college for the first time are school teaching, business, the arts, nursing, and the allied health professions. One additional career, homemaking, is endorsed by only a small percentage (.7 percent) of women entering college, but it gains substantially in popularity after college entry, so that 3.9 percent of the women plan to become homemakers four years after college entry (Astin 1977b).

The last two columns of Table 6.6 suggest dramatic changes in women's career preferences during the past ten years. These trends reflect in part the impact of the women's movement. For example, since the late 1960s, women have shown a steadily increasing interest in four occupations traditionally dominated by men: business, medicine, engineering, and law (Figure 6.2). Men's interest in these same occupations has either remained stable or declined slightly. Ten years ago women accounted for only one in nine students planning to enter these four occupations; by 1976 they accounted for more than one in three. The increase began in 1969 and 1970, about the same time that the women's movement gained momentum. These increases are still accelerating. In just the seven years since 1969 they have been impressive in all four fields: the percentage planning to enter business has tripled (from 4 percent to 12 percent), the percentage planning to become doctors has more than doubled (from 1.3 percent to 3.3 percent), the percentage planning to become lawyers has more than tripled (from .8 percent to 3 percent), and the percentage planning to become engineers has increased fivefold (from .3 percent to 1.5 percent). Although follow-up studies indicated that women are somewhat more likely than men to drop out of these fields during the undergraduate years, these dramatic changes in career preferences of entering college women may ultimately have a profound effect on the labor force and on these four professions. One possibility is that the quality of professional practice, particularly in medicine and law, may improve. Both professions require a considerable amount of empathy and interpersonal sensitivity, traits that research on sex differences has shown are more characteristic of women than of men. Increasing the number of women lawyers will, of course, expand the base of women candidates qualified for public office.

TABLE 6.6

Changes in Career Choices of Freshman Women
and Men, 1976

Career Choice	Women	Men	Change Since 1966	
			Women	Men
Artist	8	6	- 1	+ 1
Businessman	12	21	+ 9	+ 2
Clergy and Religious Workers	0	1	- 1	0
College Teacher	0	0	- 2	- 2
Doctor (M.D. or D.D.S.)	3	6	+ 1	- 1
Educator (secondary)	4	3	-14	- 8
Educator (elementary)	8	1	- 8	0
Engineer	2	14	+ 2	- 2
Farmer or Forester	1	5	+ 1	+ 2
Health Professional (non-M.D.)	11	4	+ 4	+ 1
Lawyer	3	6	+ 2	- 1
Nurse	9	0	+ 4	0
Research Scientist	2	3	0	- 2
Other Occupation	25	21	- 6	+ 5
Undecided	11	10	+ 7	+ 5

Source: Compiled by the author.

How do women's career plans change once they enter college? Four- and five-year follow-ups of the 1968 and 1969 entering classes (Astin, 1977b) provide some clues about influences on women's career plans after college entry. Women are somewhat more likely

than men to abandon their initial plans to pursue traditionally masculine careers such as medicine and law, whereas men are more
likely than women to leave the traditionally feminine career of
school teaching. Moreover, about one-fourth of the women who initially plan to become either school teachers or nurses switch to
homemaking within four or five years after entering college. These
longitudinal results were obtained during the late 1960s and early
1970s. More recent entering women may or may not be equally inclined to drop out of so-called masculine fields and to leave teaching and nursing for homemaking. If the trends in plans of successive freshman classes are any indication, future follow-ups will
show a somewhat different pattern of change after college entry.

The principal influence on women to abandon plans for teaching is a decision to get married (Astin, 1977b). Marriage, however,
has no effect on a man's chances of implementing plans to teach.
This discrepancy is consistent with a recent national study of college dropouts (Astin 1975) which reveals that marriage has a negative effect of a woman's chances of finishing college and a positive
effect on a man's chances. It would be useful to determine from
future follow-ups of more recent entering classes if these sex differences pertaining to the effects of marriage on career are still
operating.

How do women fare in the competition for jobs once they complete their undergraduate education? A 1974 follow-up of 1969 entering freshmen (Astin 1975) provided an opportunity to compare the
jobs obtained by women and men in business and teaching. After
the students' personal background (ability, family income, education) and educational experience (undergraduate grades, type of college attended) are considered, women who take jobs in business or
teaching start with substantially lower salaries than men. In business, being a man is worth approximately $1,900 in additional
salary. Among students taking jobs as teachers, being a man is
worth approximately $1,100 in additional salary. Why women
should receive lower salaries than men with comparable characteristics is not entirely clear. One explanation is outright sex discrimination: businesses and schools may be less willing to pay
women comparable salaries. Another possibility is that women
may be more willing to settle for lower salaries, particularly if
their mobility is restricted by their husbands' careers. Women
may seek lower-paying jobs. In business, for example, men may
be more interested in sales jobs, which probably pay more, whereas
women may be more likely to select office jobs. Similarly, men
may be more likely to seek teaching jobs in higher paying schools
(secondary rather than elementary, for example). Whatever the
explanation, this large discrepancy in the starting salaries of women

and men merits much more intensive study to assess the relative importance of motivation, sex discrimination, and other factors.

Surveys of entering college students show clearly that women are less interested in early marriage and increasingly motivated to pursue careers in fields that have traditionally been dominated by men: medicine, law, business, and engineering. If one looks ahead to the next 15 or 20 years, these trends suggest the possibility of profound changes in American society. It is interesting, for example, to speculate on how the quality of medical practice would change if more doctors were altruistic and empathic and fewer were either competitive or status-oriented. Similarly, a substantial influx of women into law and business could have a major impact on the style and quality of leadership and professional performance in such critical areas as the courts, legislatures, politics, business, and industry.

Perhaps the most surprising finding from the longitudinal follow-ups was the apparent failure of the undergraduate experience to reduce stereotypic differences between the sexes. If anything, these differences tend to become somewhat neater after students enter college. One obvious factor is the curriculum: women are much more likely to major in fields like literature and the arts, whereas men more often major in the sciences and engineering. Another, more subtle factor is that college faculties and, in particular, college administrations are controlled by men (Astin 1977a). This predominantly male orientation is no doubt responsible for the considerable emphasis many colleges give to athletics, achievement, and competition. Men entering college are provided with strong reinforcement for their stereotypic masculine traits. Women, however, would be less likely to acquire such traits, given the absence of potential role models among the faculty and administration.

SUMMARY

The major findings from national surveys of college students as they relate to the educational development of women undergraduates indicate that at college entry women exhibit a number of stereotypic differences in attitudes, behavior, and aspirations. Compared with men, women undergraduates are more altruistic, liberal, cooperative, religious, and empathic, and less competitive, aggressive, and hedonistic. They are more likely to pursue careers in teaching, nursing, and the arts, and less likely to go into science, business, law, and medicine. Their greater studiousness is reflected in higher grades, but their greater propensity for early marriage frequently results in a decision to drop out of college.

Longitudinal follow-ups suggest that the experience of college attendance contributes little to the reduction of these stereotypic sex differences. With the exception of political liberalism, where men's and women's views converge during the college years, most sex differences are not eliminated or even reduced by the undergraduate experience. One might expect that the common experience of attending college, where both women and men take similar courses and are exposed to the same professors, would tend to reduce some sex differences over time, but such is seldom the case. The experience of attending college actually preserves more than reduces stereotypic differences between men and women in behavior, personality, aspiration, and achievement.

Recent evidence from surveys of entering classes suggests that many differences between the sexes have narrowed during the past few years. Perhaps most dramatic is the change in women's career plans and educational aspirations. Women are increasingly disinclined to opt for careers in traditionally feminine fields (school teaching in particular) and now represent more than one-third of all freshmen aspiring to traditionally masculine careers such as engineering, medicine, law, and business. At the same time both sexes support to a greater extent job equality for women and reject the traditional view that the proper place for married women is with the home and family. The timing of these changes in attitudes and career aspirations leaves little doubt that they are directly attributable to the impact of the women's movement.

REFERENCES

Astin, A. W. The College Environment. Washington, D.C.: American Council on Education, 1968.

Astin, A. W. Preventing Students from Dropping Out. San Francisco: Jossey-Bass, 1975.

Astin, A. W. "Hard Core of Sexism in Academe." UCLA Educator 19 (1977a): 8-18.

Astin, A. W. Four Critical Years. San Francisco: Jossey-Bass, 1977b.

Astin, A. W., Astin, H. S., Bayer, A. E., and Bisconti, A. S. The Power of Protest. San Francisco: Jossey-Bass, 1975.

Astin, A. W., and Panos, R. J. The Educational and Vocational Development of College Students. Washington, D.C.: American Council on Education, 1969.

Bayer, A. E. "Marriage Plans and Educational Aspirations." American Journal of Sociology 75 (1969): 239-44.

Chickering, A. W. Education and Identity. San Francisco: Jossey-Bass, 1969.

Horner, M. "Sex Differences in Achievement Motivation and Performance in Competitive and Noncompetitive Situations." Ph.D. dissertation, University of Michigan, Ann Arbor, 1968.

Solmon, L. C., and Taubman, P. J. Does College Matter? New York: Academic Press, 1973.

7

University Behavior and Policies: Where are the Women and Why?

Margaret Gordon
Clark Kerr

Women's long struggle for equal opportunity in higher education is fully documented in many aspects. Much historical literature sheds light primarily on the development of women's colleges and the lives of the remarkable women who fought for their establishment and led them as presidents. Much has also been written about the battles to gain admission for women students in the colleges and universities originally established for men.

The definitive history of female participation on university faculties, however, has yet to be written. Biographies of distinguished women who have taught in universities are helpful. Jessie Bernard noted that, in the first two decades of the present century, women began to join the faculties of land-grant colleges through their pioneering work in developing home economics departments. She also illuminated the distinction between the academic woman (often unmarried in the early days) who gained true professional status, and the women (usually married) who never acquired more than a marginal status as an instructor or lecturer. She called the latter a status on the fringe of the profession:

> . . . it implies also, however, that the person occupying this status is of great benefit to the institution where the work is done. There may be occasional men in this status, but by far the majority are women. For the most part, they are the wives of deans, professors, instructors, graduate students or, often, even of townsmen. They occupy an elastic labor pool, hired and furloughed as needed. They carry a large share of the backbreaking load of introductory work in English composition, modern languages, history, mathematics, natural sciences, and the like. (Bernard 1964, p. 100)

Yet there were women who became professors in universities in fields other than home economics. What fields were they in, and what were the characteristics of the universities that gave them their opportunities? Was it simply a case of particularly remarkable individual women who somehow managed to gain recognition despite the pervasive atmosphere of male domination of university faculties, or were there certain fields in which they were likely to be found and certain types of universities that were in the vanguard in appointing women to their faculties? Those questions are difficult to answer.

However, much can be learned about the history of women on a university campus from a study of early catalogs. A perusal of catalogs for the University of California at Berkeley (UCB), gave quite a clear picture of women's position on that campus. Personal memories of prominent women members of the Berkeley faculty in the 1930s and later add details to the picture.

HISTORICAL OVERVIEW OF WOMEN AT BERKELEY

Whatever its early history, in recent decades Berkeley has not been noted for a large proportion of women on its faculty. When Berkeley presented its affirmative action plan to the Department of Health, Education, and Welfare in spring 1975, 6.5 percent of its ladder faculty was women (Table 7.1). This percentage was far lower than the 14.9 percent (computed from data in Table 7.2) reported by the National Center for Education Statistics (NCES) for all universities in the 1974-75 academic year. In fact, Berkeley fell into the expected pattern of the prestigious university.

The report of the Subcommittee on the Status of Academic Women at Berkeley, presented to the Academic Senate in 1970, indicated that "the representation of women on the Berkeley Academic Senate was less in 1969 than it was twenty years earlier, or for that matter forty years earlier." The report said:

> The percentage of women professors has gone down to 2% of all professors, though it was more than 4% in the 1950s. The percentage of women associate professors has decreased to 5%. At both steps, the proportion of women is now comparable to that of the 1920s. The decrease in the proportion of women assistant professors is even more striking and more ominous for the future. Only 5% are women, which is half the figure of the early twenties and less than one-third the percentage for the period 1925-45. (UCB 1970, p. 6)

TABLE 7.1

Ladder Faculty Members by Field and Sex, 1900–01 to 1974–75

Field	Men (N)	Women (N)	Women (percent)	Men (N)	Women (N)	Women (percent)	Men (N)	Women (N)	Women (percent)	Men (N)	Women (N)	Women (percent)
Total	64	0	0	298	12	3.9	431	27	5.9	1,394	97	6.5
Arts	0	0	0	1	0	0	7	0	0	43	0	0
Humanities	18	0	0	57	2	3.4	82	2	2.3	209	24	10.3
Social sciences	6	0	0	26	3	10.3	50	5	9.0	209	17	7.5
Ethnic studies	0	0	0	0	0	0	0	0	0	5	2	28.6
Biological sciences	8	0	0	27	2	6.9	37	3	7.5	135	23	14.6
Physical sciences	9	0	0	21	0	0	44	2	4.3	166	2	1.2
Health sciences	0	0	0	2	2	50.0	4	5	55.6	34	5	12.8
Natural resources (professional)	7	0	0	99	3	2.9	98	5	4.9	94	8	7.8
Physical sciences (professional)	10	0	0	36	0	0	54	0	0	267	2	0.7
Social sciences (professional)	2	0	0	8	0	0	16	4	20.0	135	7	4.9
Environmental design	0	0	0	4	0	0	7	0	0	66	5	7.0
Law (professional)	3	0	0	8	0	0	12	1	7.7	31	2	6.1
Military science	1	0	0	9	0	0	20	0	0	0	0	0

Source: Data are from University of California, Berkeley, catalogs for the selected dates, and from Affirmative Action Program and Related Documents vol. 1. Berkeley: University of California, February 1975.

TABLE 7.2

Women as a Percentage of Full-Time Faculty Members,
by Rank and Type of Institution, 1972-73 to 1975-76

Institution and Rank	1972-73	1974-75	1975-76
All institutions	22.3	24.1	24.2
Professors	9.8	10.3	9.8
Associate professors	16.3	16.9	16.8
Assistant professors	23.8	27.1	28.6
Instructors and other	38.0	39.4	39.3
Universities	16.4	18.5	18.2
Professors	6.3	6.3	6.0
Associate professors	12.5	13.3	13.2
Assistant professors	19.8	23.9	25.4
Instructors and other	44.4	46.4	45.4
Other four-year institutions	23.4	25.0	24.8
Professors	12.5	12.9	12.3
Associate professors	18.1	18.7	18.4
Assistant professors	25.1	28.1	19.8
Instructors and other	43.1	45.5	47.1
Two-year institutions	32.9	33.3	33.4
Professors	22.1	24.8	23.3
Associate professors	25.0	24.9	25.2
Assistant professors	31.9	34.4	35.5
Instructors and other	35.9	34.9	34.9

Source: Percentages for 1972-73 and 1973-74 from Making Affirmative Action Work in Higher Education: An Analysis of Institutional and Federal Policies with Recommendations, by the Carnegie Council on Higher Education. San Francisco: Jossey-Bass, 1975, pp. 21-22. Percentages for 1975-76 from "Women Faculty Lose a Little More Ground, NCES Reports," Higher Education Daily 2 February 1976.

A table showed the number of men and women in faculty ladder positions at ten-year intervals from 1928-29 to 1968-69. These data, however, were incomplete. According to Lucy Mitchell (1953) the first dean of women, she and Jessica Peixotto, both appointed to regular faculty ranks in 1906, were the first women on the faculty. Thus, the Berkeley catalogue for 1900-01 showed 64 men and no women in ladder ranks (Table 7.1). In those days the university relied more heavily on instructors than it has recently, but all 41 instructors listed in the catalogue seem to be men.

Using catalogues to identify the sex of faculty members presented some difficulties. Some names--for example, Meredith--could not be positively identified as male or female. Early catalogues sometimes gave only initials, but for those early years it seemed safe to assume that those individuals were men. Recently, the chief difficulty arose from the large number of joint appointments, which resulted in listing some faculty members in two or more departments.

By 1921-22, 12 women were in ladder positions, about equally divided between those departments where one would expect to find women and those where their presence was somewhat surprising. Two women were in physical education for women, and three were in home economics. There were also two women in hygiene, one listed as assistant professor of hygiene and physician for women and the other as assistant professor of public health nursing--not unexpected positions for women. Somewhat less expected were two women in public speaking and two in economics (one was Jessica Peixotto). There was also a female associate clinical professor of abnormal psychology, not altogether a surprise in view of the large number of women in clinical psychology today.

If the doors of the regular faculty were barely open to women in 1921-22, however, women were beginning to play a much more important role as instructors, lecturers, assistants, and the like. The departmental faculty lists included 225 people in such categories in 1921-22; 63 or 28 percent were women.

By 1930-31, the total ladder faculty at Berkeley had grown to 458; 27 or 5.9 percent were women. The number of women in home economics had increased to five, as had the number in hygiene. A woman appeared in the German department. The number of women in ladder positions in economics grew to four, a surprise, for economics was then and still is predominantly a male field. One explanation may have been the influence of Jessica Peixotto, who had strong interests (as do women in economics today) in consumer economics and what was then called social economics, which included the economics of poverty. She probably played a role in attracting other women with similar interests.

Another surprise was the presence of a female associate professor; she later became a full professor in the law school. The first woman law professor in the country, Barbara Nachtrieb Armstrong was attractive, brilliant, and dynamic. An untiring battler for social justice, she wrote a pioneering book on social insurance in industrial countries (Armstrong 1932).

In both the economics department and the law school, however, the personalities and interests of some of the men probably helped make these women welcome. In 1930 several members of the economics department, particularly Paul S. Taylor, were noted for their broad social concerns more than for their contributions to economic analysis. Taylor was an expert on farm labor problems and, in the period of the Okies and Arkies, attracted able graduate students who wrote Ph.D. theses on the plight of the farm workers. The law school had Max Radin, a liberally educated, charming legal scholar, and Roger J. Traynor, who later had a distinguished career as a member and eventually chief justice of the California Supreme Court.

Thus the early breakthroughs of women on the Berkeley faculty are explained partly by their appearance in such fields as home economics and physical education, partly by some outstanding women, and partly by the unusual characteristics of the departments that hired them. However, Berkeley was not a promising place for women. It was a land-grant institution with a large proportion of its faculty in agriculture, forestry, and engineering. These three fields accounted for nearly 40 percent of the entire ladder faculty in 1921 and for about 30 percent in 1930. Even today some of the most exclusively male faculties are in land-grant institutions.

During the 1930s and after World War II Berkeley evolved from a somewhat provincial campus to one of the most distinguished universities in the country. It was the leader in two surveys of the quality of graduate education (Cartter 1966; Roos & Andersen 1970), renowned in physical sciences and engineering. Since these two fields did not attract women, it is not surprising that the proportion of women faculty members declined between the 1930s and the 1960s. However, many departments, not only in traditionally male fields but also in the humanities and social sciences, have continued to be entirely male.

WOMEN ON UNIVERSITY FACULTIES TODAY

Women are less likely to hold positions on the faculties of universities than of four- or two-year colleges (Table 7.2). Although their proportion among university faculties has increased modestly in the last few years, the gains have been almost entirely at the assistant professor and instructor level. In fact, the percentages of women among full and associate professors dropped slightly between 1974-75 and 1975-76.

Apparently the more prestigious the university, the smaller the percentage of women among its faculty members. Surveys by women's professional groups in particular fields--for example, chemistry, economics, and sociology--have revealed few or no women in the most prestigious departments in those fields (Carnegie Council on Higher Education 1975; Carnegie Commission on Higher Education 1973b).

Data from the annual salary survey of the American Association of University Professors (AAUP) for 1975-76 were useful in exploring the variations in the inclusion of women on university faculties. The survey provides information on the number of full-time faculty members by sex in the ranks of full professor, associate professor, assistant professor, and instructor. The percentage of women among full professors reflects the results of hiring and promotional patterns in the postwar period, whereas data on lower ranks reflect recent hiring patterns.

Using the Carnegie Commission on Higher Education classification of institutions of higher education (1973a), we do indeed find that the percentage of women among full professors is smallest in the most prestigious group, Research Universities I, and tends to rise with the declining prestige of the institutions (Table 7.3). Moreover, it is distinctly smaller in private than in public institutions, not only in universities, but also in the four subclassifications of universities.

TABLE 7.3

Women as a Percentage of Full-Time Full Professors
in Universities, by Carnegie Classification
and Control, 1975-76

Carnegie Classification	Total	Public	Private
Total	6.0	6.3	4.9
Research Universities I	4.5	4.7	3.9
Research Universities II	6.1	6.2	5.7
Ph.D.-granting Universities I	6.2	6.4	5.5
Ph.D.-granting Universities II	10.2	10.8	8.7

Note: Percentages are weighted averages, that is, the total number of women faculty in each group of institutions was divided by the total number of faculty in each group.

Source: Percentages computed from "Nearly Keeping Up: The Economic Status of the Profession, 1975-76," AAUP Bulletin (August 1976): 195-284.

The averages in Table 7.3 conceal wide variations among the institutions included in the subcategories. Clues to these variations can be found by studying the extremes. Table 7.4 provides data on the 20 universities with the largest percentages of women and the 20 institutions with the smallest percentages. Texas Woman's University, with the largest percentage of women on its faculty, is the only women's institution in the group. The others with comparatively large percentages appear to have one or both of two characteristics: either they are located in the inner city of a large metropolitan area or they are former teachers colleges with large proportions of students enrolled in education and sometimes in other predominantly female fields.

The universities with the fewest women on their faculties have quite different characteristics: they were sometimes formerly male institutions; they are often oriented toward science and engineering (if they are land-grant institutions, toward agriculture as well); and they are not located in the inner cities, but may be located in small communities.

In the public universities, the percentage of women among full professors varied directly with the percentage of women among the students (Table 7.5). Faculty members, male or female, are more likely to recommend women for appointment when there will be a substantial number of women students in classes. Moreover, some universities with large percentages of women students (especially those with 50 percent or more) are former teachers colleges with heavy enrollments in education. Qualified women are usually available in education. In the private universities, also, there is a consistent pronounced relationship between the percentage of women among full professors and the percentage among students (Table 7.6).

Thirty-nine of the universities were in the inner city of a metropolitan area with a population of 1 million or more. The majority, or nearly 60 percent, had percentages of women among their full professors which exceeded the average for their Carnegie category, public or private, in some cases by a substantial margin. This relationship is consistent with Solmon's (1973) finding that women graduate students are more concentrated in universities in large urban centers than are men graduate students. Solmon indicated that married women living in large urban areas and wishing to do graduate work were especially likely to enroll in a large city university because their husbands worked in the area and they were not free to move. Similarly, qualified married women living in a large urban area will probably accept teaching positions in urban universities.

TABLE 7.4

Women as a Percentage of Full-Time Full Professors in Universities with the Highest and the Lowest Percentages of Women, 1975-76

Universities	Percent Full Professors
Highest Percentage	
Texas Woman's University	43.6
Adelphi University	22.4
Howard University	16.9
Ball State University	15.4
University of Northern Colorado	15.2
Fordham University	14.8
University of Louisville	13.7
North Dakota State University	13.0
Northern Illinois University	12.7
Bowling Green State University	12.6
Wayne State University	12.5
Virginia Commonwealth University	12.4
University of Wisconsin, Milwaukee	12.1
Texas Christian University	11.1
Illinois State University	11.0
Florida State University	10.6
Temple University	10.5
Rutgers--The State University	10.0
Great Western Reserve University	9.9
University of North Dakota	9.9
Lowest Percentage	
Rockefeller University	0.0
University of Notre Dame	0.0
Georgia Institute of Technology	0.0
North Carolina State University	0.4
Texas A&M University	0.7
Princeton University	0.7
Emory University	1.2
Utah State University	1.2
Carnegie-Mellon University	1.2
Clemson University	1.4
University of New Hampshire	1.5
Vanderbilt University	1.6
Brown University	1.6
Lehigh University	1.6
Yale University	1.7
University of Kentucky	1.7
University of Delaware	1.8
Stanford University	1.9
University of California, Irvine	1.9
Massachusetts Institute of Technology	2.0

Source: Percentages computed from "Nearly Keeping Up: The Economic Status of the Profession, 1975-76," AAUP Bulletin (August 1976): 195-284.

TABLE 7.5

Women as a Percentage of Full Professors in Public Universities by
Women as a Percentage of Students, 1975–76

Percentage of Full Professors	Percentage of Students*						
	0–19.9	20.0–29.9	30.0–34.9	35.0–39.9	40.0–44.9	45.0–49.9	50.0 and over
0–0.9	1	2					
1.0–1.9				2	3	1	
2.0–2.9			1	2	4		
3.0–3.9				5	1		1
4.0–4.9				3	7	1	
5.0–5.9			1	3	12	3	
6.0–6.9			1	1	8	2	
7.0–7.9				1	2	2	
8.0–8.9						2	
9.0–9.9					1		1
10.0–14.9				1	3	3	4
15.0 and over					1		3
Average (unweighted)	0.0	0.6	4.9	4.6	5.6	7.2	15.1

*Student data for 1974–75.

Source: Percentages computed from "Nearly Keeping Up: The Economic Status of the Profession, 1975–76," AAUP Bulletin (August 1976): 195–284; and from Higher Education: Fall Enrollment in Higher Education, 1974 (Table 19). Washington, D.C.: NCES, 1975.

TABLE 7.6

Women as a Percentage of Full Professors in Private
Universities, by Women as a Percentage
of Students, 1975-76

Percentage of Full Professors	Percentage of Students*				
	0-19.9	20.0-29.9	30.0-39.9	40.0-49.9	50.0 and Over
0-1.9	1	4	5		
2.0-2.9	1	1	1		
3.0-3.9				1	
4.0-4.9		1	6	1	
5.0-5.9			3	2	
6.0-6.9			2	1	
7.0-7.9				1	
8.0-8.9			2	4	
9.0-9.9			2	1	
10.0-14.9			1	1	
15.0 and over				1	1
Average (unweighted)	1.0	1.6	5.2	8.0	22.4

*Student data for 1974-75.
Source: Percentages computed from "Nearly Keeping Up: The Economic Status of the Profession, 1975-76," AAUP Bulletin (August 1976): 195-284; and Higher Education: Fall Enrollment in Higher Education, 1974, Table 19. Washington, D.C.: NCES, 1975.

To test the predominance of traditionally male fields of study in the 20 universities with the smallest percentages of women on their faculties, the proportion of B.A. degrees the institutions awarded in agriculture and natural resources, biological sciences, engineering, and physical sciences in 1971-72 (the latest year for which data were available), was computed. In the case of Rockefeller University, exclusively a graduate institution, the proportion of Ph.D.s was computed. Eight of the 20 institutions granted more than 30 percent of their degrees in traditionally male fields:

University	Percentage
Rockefeller University	89.5
Massachusetts Institute of Technology	64.8
Georgia Institute of Technology	62.0
North Carolina State University	58.4
Lehigh University	50.6
Texas A&M University	46.5
Carnegie-Mellon University	36.6
Clemson University	32.5

However, of the 20 universities with the largest proportion of women among their faculty members, 15 granted unusually large proportions of their B.A. degrees in education, home economics, letters, library science, and social work (with the percentage of education degrees accounting for the largest proportion in most instances):

University	Percentage
Illinois State University	59.2
University of Northern Colorado	57.4
Ball State University	55.4
Bowling Green State University	52.1
Texas Woman's University	50.2
Northern Illinois University	47.6
University of North Dakota	42.7
University of Wisconsin, Milwaukee	41.6
Florida State University	40.2
Temple University	38.7
Wayne State University	36.0
Adelphi University	32.3
North Dakota State University	29.7
Virginia Commonwealth University	29.4
Texas Christian University	28.4

Without exception, the percentage of women among assistant professors in the universities responding to the American Association of University Professors (AAUP) survey was much higher than the proportion of women in the full professor category. The proportion of women among associate professors also tended to be higher, although by a smaller margin.

All in all, 13.5 percent of the full-time ladder faculty members in the universities in 1975-76 were women (Table 7.7). This exceeds the percentage of women among Ph.D. recipients in the late 1960s (about 11 percent), but is smaller than the average percentage of women among Ph.D. recipients from 1970 to 1976 (about 17 percent).

Moreover, the proportion of women among Ph. D. recipients has been rising at a rapid rate, from 13.3 percent in 1970 to an estimated 21.1 percent in 1976 (NCES 1976). However, as Table 7.2 indicates, the percentage of women among assistant professors in universities in 1975-76--the clearest indicator of recent hiring patterns--was 25.4 percent. The universities were probably hiring some women who had received their Ph. D. s some time ago; they may also have been hiring women who had not yet received the Ph. D.

TABLE 7.7

Women as a Percentage of Full-Time Ladder Faculty
Members in Universities, by Carnegie
Classification and Control, 1975-76

Carnegie Classification	Total	Public	Private
Total	13.5	13.5	13.5
Research Universities I	11.2	11.2	11.2
Research Universities II	14.3	14.4	13.9
Ph. D.-granting Universities I	14.6	14.4	15.3
Ph. D.-granting Universities II	19.4	19.2	19.9

Note: Percentages are weighted averages, that is, the total number of women faculty in each group of institutions was divided by the total number of faculty in each group.
Source: Percentages computed from "Nearly Keeping Up: The Economic Status of the Profession, 1975-76," AAUP Bulletin (August 1976): 195-284.

The variations among Carnegie categories of universities, public and private, in the proportions of women in the ladder faculty group followed much the same pattern as that for the full professor level. But the variations were somewhat narrower, and the data suggest that the institutions with the smallest percentages of women among their full professors were making a special effort to hire women at lower levels.

Table 7.8 provides a rough indication of such a tendency. Data indicate that the ratio of women among ladder faculty to women among full professors was larger in private than in public institutions, not only as a whole, but also in each of the Carnegie categories.

Furthermore, the ratios were higher in Research Universities I than in the other categories and tended to decline with declining prestige by Carnegie type. This convergence suggests that the old pattern of fewest women in the most prestigious institutions may eventually disappear.

TABLE 7.8

Ratio of Percentage of Women Among Full-Time Ladder
Faculty to Percentage Among Full-Time Professors in
Universities, by Carnegie Classification
and Control, 1975-76

Carnegie Classification	Total	Public	Private
Total	2.98	2.84	3.28
Research Universities I	3.48	3.26	3.85
Research Universities II	2.80	2.62	3.21
Ph.D.-granting Universities I	3.03	3.01	3.09
Ph.D.-granting Universities II	2.23	2.07	2.51

Note: Percentages are weighted averages, that is, the total number of women faculty in each group of institutions was divided by the total number of faculty in each group.
Source: Percentages computed from "Nearly Keeping Up: The Economic Status of the Profession, 1975-76," AAUP Bulletin (August 1976): 195-184.

Another view of this convergence is provided by Table 7.9, which shows the universities with the highest ratios of the percentage of women among ladder faculty to the percentage of women among full professors. Institutions with the highest ratios have the lowest percentages of women in full professorships. Table 7.9 is an honor roll for effort: it should also include Rockefeller University, Georgia Institute of Technology, and the University of Notre Dame, for which ratios could not be computed because they had no women among their full professors. However, they had hired women in the lower ranks.

Summing up, we have shown that the percentages of women on faculties of universities do tend to vary inversely with the prestige of the institution, but that the variations are not related to prestige

TABLE 7.9

Universities in which Ratio of Women among Full-Time Ladder
Faculty Exceeds Ratio among Full-Time Full Professors
by More than 3.5:1.0, 1975-76

University	Percentage of Women Among Full Professors (1)	Percentage of Women Among Ladder Faculty (2)	Ratio of (2) : (1)
North Carolina State University	0.4	6.5	16.20
Princeton University	0.7	7.9	11.52
University of Delaware	1.8	17.3	9.71
University of New Hampshire	1.5	11.5	7.79
Clemson University	1.4	9.4	6.88
Utah State University	1.2	8.2	6.72
Yale University	1.7	10.7	6.17
Vanderbilt University	1.6	10.0	6.16
Carnegie-Mellon University	1.2	7.4	5.96
University of Kentucky	1.7	10.2	5.90
University of Vermont	3.1	17.5	5.68
Emory University	1.2	6.7	5.53
University of Utah	2.8	13.6	4.91
Ohio University	2.3	11.0	4.76
University of California, Irvine	1.9	8.8	4.67
United States International University	4.0	18.6	4.66
New Mexico State University	2.6	11.6	4.47
Texas A&M University	0.7	2.9	4.36
University of North Carolina	3.9	16.4	4.25
Stanford University	1.9	7.8	4.22
Brown University	1.6	6.8	4.20
Georgetown University	4.2	17.1	4.11
Northeastern University	5.2	21.1	4.10
University of California, San Diego	2.2	9.2	4.09
University of Maine	2.5	10.3	4.06
Rice University	2.2	8.7	4.04
Lehigh University	1.6	6.1	3.82
University of Tulsa	4.5	16.9	3.73
Harvard University	2.4	9.1	3.71
Massachusetts Institute of Technology	2.0	7.2	3.65
University of Akron	4.5	16.3	3.61

Source: Compiled by the authors.

alone. In particular, among the most prestigious universities there are a number of the formerly all-male private universities and some of the heavily science-oriented land-grant institutions, while among the more modest of the Ph. D.-granting institutions are a number of former teachers colleges with strong emphasis on awarding degrees in education. Differences in proportions of women on faculties are related to these characteristics as well as to prestige.

POLICY IMPLICATIONS

Women active in the movement to improve their status in higher education tend to complain that little or no progress has been made under the recent federal affirmative action policies. Their complaints are based on evidence (such as that in Table 7.2) showing that the only pronounced changes in the sexual composition of faculties have occurred at the assistant professor and instructor levels. Actually this is inevitable, since new hiring occurs at the lower ranks.

The data provide a somewhat fuller view of events in universities, indicating that women are being added to faculties among these institutions and that the most pronounced changes are taking place in the faculties that were formerly almost entirely male.

It is too early to determine whether the lack of progress at the full professor level reflects the influence of old prejudices against women rising through the professorial ranks. The normal period required for a newly hired assistant professor to be promoted to associate professor is about six years. Enforcement of federal affirmative action policies for women in higher education dates only from 1970; these policies did not become active until 1972 or later (Carnegie Commission on Higher Education 1973b). Moreover, the increase in the percentage of women among professors did not begin until about 1972. Meanwhile, as Fulton (1975) has shown, in 1969 there were more women among faculty members aged 55 and over than in all other age groups except the youngest (who would be mostly instructors). This comparatively elderly age distribution of female faculty members was the heritage of the decline in the proportion of women on faculties after the 1930s. Since 1969 many of these older women have been retiring; this fact could well explain the decline in the percentage of women among full professors between 1974-75 and 1975-76 shown in Table 7.2.

Data from the University of California statewide and from the Berkeley campus (University of California Academic Senate, Berkeley Division 1970) on recent promotion rates for men and women indicate that, on a statewide basis, 20.1 percent of the men, compared with 9.3 percent of the women, who were assistant professors in October 1976 received promotions to associate professor, effective July 1977. Among those who were associate professors in October 1976, 14.4 percent of the men and 9.8 percent of the women were promoted to full professor. The Berkeley data, which relate to promotions effective July 1975 and July 1976 combined, are more encouraging. Among assistant professors, 15.5 percent of the men and 10.1 percent of the women were promoted to associate professor, while 14.6 percent of male and 14.0 percent of female associate professors were promoted to full professor. The data are not conclusive, however, because pronounced increases in the number of women appointed assistant professors have been comparatively recent. On the average, women are probably at lower steps than men within both the assistant professor and associate professor ranges.

By 1980, higher education should have a better indication of whether the recent upsurge in the proportion of women among assistant professors will result in more women moving into the higher ranks. University policies to ensure that there is no discrimination against women in promotion decisions will be critical. Without repeating all the recommendations made by the Carnegie Commission on Higher Education (1973b) and the Carnegie Council on Higher Education (1975), achievement of this objective depends on the involvement of all those concerned within the institution: the board of trustees, the administration, and all faculty members participating in promotion decisions.

Beyond this, it is important to recognize that in the very age range when assistant professors are achieving the record that will determine their success in gaining promotion, about age 25 to 35, married women are likely to be bearing and rearing their children (Carnegie Commission on Higher Education 1973b). These policies will, of course, delay promotion for women with family responsibilities, but they will often be crucial in determining a woman's ultimate success in gaining distinction in her field.

The data also underscore the decisive role of traditionally male and female fields in determining the presence or absence of women faculty members. Few women have held faculty positions in traditionally male fields in universities. However, few people have been aware of the role of these differences in explaining variations among universities in the sexual composition of their faculties.

The Carnegie Council on Higher Education (1975) stressed the importance of increasing the supply of women and minorities who were qualified for faculty appointments, as well as eliminating discrimination on the demand side. The emphasis on increasing supply was never disputed for minorities, but it was attacked rather frequently by women's groups. Some attacks implied that the council recommended efforts only on the supply side, ignoring the fact that most of the report was concerned with ways to make affirmative action policies more effective on the demand side. Frequently spokespersons for women's groups protested that there were qualified women who were not being hired, citing the data, for example, from the National Academy of Science 1973 survey of Ph.D. scientists and engineers that 3.9 percent of the women, compared with only 0.9 percent of the men, were unemployed (Wolfe 1975). However, the Carnegie Council on Higher Education was not referring to supply in relation to current demand, but rather to the supply of qualified women needed if women were to comprise a proportion of faculty members comparable to their current proportion of the labor force, about 38 percent (Carnegie Council on Higher Education 1975). Only in a few traditionally female fields do women currently receive 38 percent or more of the Ph.D.s; despite impressive progress in recent years in the natural sciences, engineering, economics, business administration, and other traditionally male fields, their percentages of the Ph.D. recipients continue to be small. Thus it is in the traditionally male fields that there is a particular supply problem for women. The Carnegie Council on Higher Education did not intend to imply that there was a need to increase the supply of women in such fields as English literature and history, in which women have been receiving larger proportions of the Ph.D.s. In 1974, for example, women received 37 percent of the Ph.D.s in English and 18 percent of those in history (Chronicle of Higher Education 1976). However, in those fields the job market outlook is particularly bleak.

The obstacles to increasing the supply of women in traditionally male fields originate in the cultural influences and educational practices that affect girls from infancy onward, as the Carnegie Commission on Higher Education (1973b) made clear. Particularly critical, Lucy Sells (1974) noted, are the influences that deter women in high school from continuing their mathematical training. Yet the recent increases in the proportions of women beginning graduate training and receiving degrees in traditionally male fields are striking.

Until the cultural and educational influences that have inhibited women from preparing for traditional male professions are fundamentally altered, one cannot know whether residual sexual differences in tastes will remain and result in continuing, but perhaps less pronounced, sexual differences in educational and career choices. The important goal is freedom of choice, and freedom of choice is not meaningful as long as financial, cultural, and social barriers interfere with the fulfillment of aspirations based on individual goals and abilities. In the short run, universities need to make strong efforts to overcome the effects of past discrimination.

In the long run, the differing tastes of men and women, and of racial and ethnic groups, may well continue to contribute to diversity in American higher education.

Disaggregation of the data on universities shows that progress is generally being made in the lower ranks, and that changes tend to be most pronounced in institutions that formerly had the fewest women on their faculties. The critical question of whether proportions of women in the high ranks will rise appreciably cannot be answered until the early 1980s. Despite the evidence of convergence, differences in the percentages of women among faculty members from university to university will undoubtedly continue. These will reflect the institutions' relative concentration in traditionally male or female fields, the sexual characteristics of their students, their location, and unique factors in their historical development.

REFERENCES

Armstrong, B. N. Insuring the Essentials: Minimum Wage Plus Social Insurance--a Living Wage Program. New York: Macmillan, 1932.

Bernard, J. Academic Women. University Park, Pa.: Pennsylvania State University Press, 1964.

Carnegie Commission on Higher Education. A Classification of Institutions of Higher Education. Berkeley: Carnegie Commission, 1973a.

Carnegie Commission on Higher Education. Opportunities for Women in Higher Education: Their Current Participation, Prospects for the Future and Recommendations for Action. New York: McGraw-Hill, 1973b.

Carnegie Council on Higher Education. Making Affirmative Action Work in Higher Education: An Analysis of Institutional and Federal Policies with Recommendations. San Francisco: Jossey-Bass, 1975.

Cartter, A. M. An Assessment of Quality in Graduate Education. Washington, D.C.: American Council on Education, 1966.

Chronicle of Higher Education. Degrees Awarded in Various Fields, 1974. July 19, 1976.

Fulton, O. "Rewards and Fairness: Academic Women in the United States." In Teachers and Students: Aspects of American Higher Education, ed. M. Trow. New York: McGraw-Hill, 1975.

Mitchell, L. S. Two Lives: The Story of Wesley Clair Mitchell and Myself. New York: Simon and Schuster, 1953.

National Center for Education Statistics (NCES). Projections of Education Statistics to 1984-85. Washington, D.C.: NCES, 1976.

Roos, K. D., and Andersen, C. J. A Rating of Graduate Programs. Washington, D.C.: American Council on Education, 1970.

Sells, L. W. Critical Points for Affirmative Action. In New Directions for Research: Toward Affirmative Action, ed. L. W. Sells. San Francisco: Jossey-Bass, 1974.

Solmon, L. C. "Women in Graduate Education: Clues and Puzzles Regarding Discrimination." Research in Higher Education 1, no. 4 (1973).

University of California Academic Senate (UCAS), Berkeley Division. Report of the Subcommittee on the Status of Academic Women on the Berkeley Campus. Berkeley: UCAS, 1970.

Wolfe, D. P. Testimony Before the Department of Labor on the Executive Order 11246, Affirmative Action Format. Washington, D.C.: American Association of University Women, 1975.

8

Factors Affecting
Women's Scholarly Productivity

Helen S. Astin

Scholarly productivity is an important index of performance in academe. The rewards, rank and salary, are based largely on productivity. Scholarship demonstrated in published works not only increases one's status, but also represents one's contributions to knowledge, the advancement of science, and the betterment of society.

Often a woman's lower status in academe has been attributed to her lower productivity rate. However, studies of productivity have demonstrated the importance of a number of institutional factors that affect scholarly productivity. These factors emerge in studies independent of sample or time. Invariably, the institution at which a person took graduate training is a significant factor in later productivity. Astin (1969) reported that, for female Ph.D.s, productivity as measured by published articles is greatly determined by the quality of the graduate institution. Women who participated in high-quality graduate programs are more likely to have published three or more scientific or scholarly articles.

Explaining the relationship of institutional quality to later productivity is a complicated task. The positive relationship may result primarily from a person's characteristics rather than from the institution attended. For example, it is likely that more achievement-oriented and creative persons select and are being selected by high-quality institutions. By the same token, it is possible that the atmosphere in a highly selective institution is conducive to increased motivation and achievement orientation, and thus a graduate of a selective institution becomes a productive scholar.

In a summary of the determinants of scientific productivity, Folger, Astin, and Bayer (1970) indicated that the training institution is an important factor in later scientific accomplishment as measured by the Citation Index.* In their study the authors assessed

---

*The Citation Index measures scholarly visibility by the number of times articles, books, or other published works are cited by researchers.

the extent to which level of ability, as illustrated by college performance, relates to later achievement, as measured by citations
by scholars. They found that no relationship obtains between academic performance and citations. However, those who attended
selective graduate institutions have a higher citation index rating.
These findings suggest that persons who attend highly selective institutions are further socialized to achieve by engaging in research
and scholarship.

Another important variable in productivity is the type of institution at which a faculty member is employed. Fulton and Trow
(1974), in a study of faculty productivity, found that persons employed at universities are more productive than those employed at
four-year colleges. The importance of teaching at a university
versus a college is further illustrated by the fact that faculty at low-
quality universities are likely to be more productive than faculty at
high-quality four-year colleges. Crane's (1965) study further sub-
stantiated this relationship. She reported that, after controlling for
the quality of the training institution, a faculty member's affiliation
with a major university is an important correlate of scholarly productivity.

One can offer a number of interpretations for relationships
between institution of affiliation and productivity. A person interested in research and publications is probably more likely to be attracted by a university than one who receives great satisfaction from
teaching and interacting with students. Productive people are also
more likely to be hired by universities. Universities more often
than four-year colleges expect their faculty to engage in research.
Often four-year colleges focus on teaching and interaction with students, while universities strive to be centers of new knowledge in
science and technology. Because of their size and resources, universities have greater facilities for research. Furthermore, granting agencies might be more willing to fund research at larger institutions with their large faculties, laboratories, libraries, and other
facilities. Thus the environment at a university is designed to facili-
tate research activities and scientific and scholarly productivity.

Discipline or area of specialization may also play an important
role in scholarly productivity. If productivity is measured by published articles and books, persons in the biological and physical
sciences are more productive than persons in social sciences,
humanities, education, or arts (Astin 1969; Fulton and Trow 1974;
Startup and Gruneberg 1976). There are some field differences,
however, depending on the type of published work. For example, if
productivity is measured solely by published articles, biological and
physical scientists have the highest productivity rates, but if productivity is measured by published books those in the humanities are

more likely to have the highest productivity rates (Astin 1969).
Nevertheless, people who are productive in general tend to have
published books as well as articles and to have presented papers,
written reports, and reviewed books (Astin 1969; Startup and
Gruneberg 1976).

Faculty rank has also been identified as a correlate of productivity. Fulton and Trow (1974) examining productivity rate during
the last two years, reported that full professors are more productive than associate and assistant professors. However, some con-
tradictory findings have emerged from a survey of faculty by Ladd
and Lipset (1976). They reported that younger faculty indicate a
stronger interest in research and that they also appear to publish
more during a given period than older faculty.

Thus the relationship of rank and productivity could be interpreted in a variety of ways. From Fulton and Trow's findings it
appears that full professors, because of their past record of productivity and visibility, may have been productive during a given period
because they may have been asked to present major addresses, to
contribute chapters to edited books, or to edit volumes of their own.
Thus their high productivity is facilitated by their past record and
general visibility. From Ladd and Lipset's findings one can conclude that younger faculty who are developing their reputations are
highly motivated to publish, since the reward structure is such that
publications play a major role in achieving rank and increasing earnings. The two studies examined publications during different time
periods: whereas the Fulton and Trow study looked at productivity
during the last two years, the Ladd and Lipset study examined publications over a five-year period.

In summary, the findings reviewed thus far indicate that the
important correlates of scholarly productivity for both male and
female faculty are quality of graduate training institution, field of
specialization, type of institution of current employment, and rank.

SEX DIFFERENCES IN PRODUCTIVITY

Some studies on productivity have focused on sex differences
in publication rates (Astin 1969; Bernard 1964; Simon, Clark, and
Galway 1967; Ladd and Lipset 1976). In general, they have reported
that women are less productive than men. Part of this lower productivity is due to lower degree attainment, since fewer women have attained the Ph.D. Some is due to the type of institution with which
women are affiliated, quite likely two- and four-year colleges.
Part is also due to women's greater interest in teaching and in
carrying heavier teaching loads. Ladd and Lipset reported that

61 percent of the women and 50 percent of the men had not published in the last two years. Some 12 percent of the women, compared with 26 percent of the men, had published at least three pieces in the last two years. Ladd and Lipset indicated that, overall, more men than women say their interests are primarily in research (28 percent of the men, 17 percent of the women). Also, women spend more time in teaching and less in research activities. These differences are attributable in part to the types of institutions that employ women. According to Ladd and Lipset, women account for only one-sixth of the faculty in high-quality research universities, but one-third in institutions of lower quality.

Despite these sex differences, Ladd and Lipset found that half of the full-time faculty have never written or edited a book, more than one-third have never published an article, and half have not published anything in the last two years. Concerning faculty attitudes toward research and publishing, they found that 71 percent of the faculty feel that the quality of undergraduate education has suffered because of extensive commitment to research. Only 32 percent agree that no one can be a good teacher unless he or she is actively involved in research.

Similar findings were also obtained by an earlier survey of faculty (Bayer 1973). Bayer reported that 39 percent of the men, compared with 60 percent of the women, have never published an article. However, 35 percent of the men, compared with 12 percent of the women, have published at least five articles. A similar pattern holds for books: 58 percent of the men, compared with 74 percent of the women, have never published a book, but 17 percent of the men, compared with 7 percent of the women, have published at least three books. Again, these patterns in scholarly productivity are strongly associated with the type of institution with which academic men and women are likely to be affiliated. Bayer found that even though 20 percent of all faculty are women, only 16.5 percent of faculty at universities are women, compared with 22 percent at two-year and four-year colleges. Moreover, fewer women than men are extensively engaged in research and writing. For example, 19 percent of the women, compared with 32 percent of the men, were engaged at least nine hours per week in research and writing during the 1972-73 survey year. The teaching load also varies for men and women: 39 percent of the women, compared with 29 percent of the men, teach 13 hours or more per week, while 21 percent of the women, compared with 16 percent of the men, carry four courses or more. Thus the sex differences in productivity are the result not only of women's heavier teaching load, but also of their institutional affiliation, specialization, and general educational attainment. Bayer found that 37 percent of the faculty men, compared with only 19 percent of the women, have obtained the Ph.D. In fields with the highest productivity, such as natural sciences, women constitute a small minority: only 4 percent of the women are in physical sciences, compared with 14 percent of the men. Women are much more heavily concentrated in education and humanities, both fields with low productivity: for example, there are 23 percent of women in education, compared with 13 percent of men, and 21 percent of women in humanities, compared with 17 percent of men. Thus the sex differences in productivity reported by Ladd and Lipset and by Bayer result in part from differences in specialization, current institutional affiliation, and teaching load.

PREDICTORS OF PRODUCTIVITY
FOR MEN AND WOMEN

The present study is designed to clarify three critical issues concerning women's scholarly productivity.

First, there are factors accounting for sex differences in productivity. Since national surveys report gross differences in publication rates between men and women, the present study attempts to provide a better understanding of the factors that are important in these differences. It also examines how differences in the career paths of men and women affect productivity.

Second, there is the role of marriage. It has been argued in the past (Lester 1974; Sowell 1975) that attributing sex differentials in rank and salary to sex discrimination can be misleading and incorrect if the analysis combines single and married women. This argument assumes that single women's career paths and achievements parallel those of men, whereas married women's lower achievement results from family constraints and responsibilities and not from discrimination. The present study tests these assumptions by examining scholarly productivity, work status, and career paths of single and married women separately.

Third, there are obstacles to women's productivity. Previous work documenting sex discrimination in academe (Astin and Bayer 1972; Bayer and Astin 1975) identified scholarly productivity as a critical factor in professorial rank and salary for both sexes. However, our understanding of factors influencing scholarly productivity is limited. The present study is thus designed to shed some light on the barriers and facilitators to women's productivity.

Sample and Procedures

This examination of scholarly productivity of faculty women
and men utilized a subsample from Bayer's (1973) study of faculty.
In the academic year 1972-73 the American Council on Education
surveyed more than 100,000 college and university faculty members
in a national representative sample of 301 institutions (80 universities, 179 four-year colleges, and 42 junior or community colleges).
For the survey, 53,034 faculty members responded, of whom 42,345
were identified as currently active teaching faculty; that is, they
were teaching at least one course at one of the 301 institutions. The
sample was weighted to represent the universe of institutions and to
correct for any response bias. Women comprised 20 percent of this
sample. All the women who held Ph.D. degrees, a total of 1,800,
were selected for analysis. A similar sample of men was also
selected by choosing every tenth man who held a Ph.D. This selection yielded 2,041 men.
    The analyses were designed to examine productivity, as mea-
sured by published articles and books, among single and married
women and men in five major disciplines: biological sciences,
physical sciences, education, social sciences, and humanities.
The faculty members were classified by their publication of one to
two articles, three or more, or none. The same classification was
used for books. The tabulations of publications by field were done
with weighted Ns to correct for sampling and response bias. The
weighted Ns were 6,741 single women and 5,916 married women,
a total of 12,657 women, and 117,480 men. * Of the women in the
original survey, 42 percent were married; of the men, 87.4 percent
were married.

Differences in Productivity

An examination of the overall productivity of women and men
indicated that, while there is a difference in favor of men, there is
no difference in the productivity of single and married women. Com-
bining all fields, 26 percent of the women, whether single or married, have not published any articles compared with only 10 percent
of the men (Table 8.1). Regarding published books, the differences

------

*The weights for men were multiplied by ten in order to give
the corrected weighted N since only a 10 percent subsample was
selected for the analyses.

TABLE 8.1

Differences in Number of Articles Published, by Sex and Field
(percent)

	None			One or Two			Three or More		
Field	Single Women (N=1,716)	Married Women (N=1,474)	Men (N=12,030)	Single Women (N=1,356)	Married Women (N=1,143)	Men (N=17,860)	Single Women (N=3,584)	Married Women (N=3,162)	Men (N=86,030)
Education	28	20	16	21	24	14	51	57	70
Biology	7	5	6	19	16	6	74	79	89
Physical sciences	19	25	3	25	16	15	57	59	82
Social sciences	20	20	12	23	18	17	57	62	70
Humanities	36	37	17	21	21	20	43	43	63
Other fields	29	25	11	14	24	16	57	51	73
Total all fields	26	26	10	20	20	15	54	55	74

Source: Compiled by the author.

TABLE 8.2

Differences in Number of Books Published, by Sex and Field
(percent)

	None			One or Two			Three or More		
Field	Single Women (N=3,815)	Married Women (N=3,080)	Men (N=55,890)	Single Women (N=1,929)	Married Women (N=1,936)	Men (N=36,140)	Single Women (N=898)	Married Women (N=802)	Men (N=24,060)
Education	50	48	35	36	34	35	13	18	30
Biology	68	67	52	28	28	31	5	5	18
Physical sciences	74	64	65	21	20	25	5	16	10
Social sciences	49	44	36	25	41	32	25	15	33
Humanities	60	54	40	30	32	37	11	14	23
Other fields	53	53	53	29	36	30	18	11	17
Total all fields	57	53	48	29	31	33	14	14	21

Source: Compiled by the author.

between men and women are not as marked: 48 percent of the men have not published any books, compared with 53 percent of the married women and 57 percent of the single women (Table 8.2).

An examination of the productivity of faculty within each of the five major fields (education, biological sciences, physical sciences, social sciences, and humanities) indicated that, independent of sex, the most productive persons for articles are those in the biological sciences, with physical sciences next, whereas those in humanities are the least productive. For books, the least productive persons are in physical and biological sciences, and the most productive are in social sciences and education. An examination of the productivity of single and married women in each major field showed that a higher proportion of married women in education, biological sciences, physical sciences, and social sciences published three or more articles. More married women in education, physical sciences, and humanities published three or more books, whereas single women in social sciences were more productive than married women. Although single and married women published about the same number of articles and books across all fields, in most specific fields married women publish somewhat more than single women. These differences between married and single women on overall productivity versus productivity within fields result from differences in the fields of married and single women (see Table 8.5) as well as in publication rates for persons in different fields.

While the findings indicated that rank relates to number of publications over time, the effect of rank per se on the rate of publication was also of interest. Table 8.3 lists the proportions of faculty members within ranks who published at least three articles or books during the last two years. Male assistant professors are less productive than either associate or full professors. Male full and associate professors are similar in overall productivity. The productivity of married women is greater with each higher rank in the major fields: assistant professors are the least productive, associate professors are next, and full professors are the most productive. The patterns for single women are more erratic: assistant and associate professors tend to be somewhat more productive than full professors. The earlier interpretation that reaching the rank of full professor is in itself beneficial because it provides for greater visibility and productivity is not valid for single women.

Within each rank and across all fields except for assistant professors in physical sciences, married women are more productive than single women. Furthermore, married female full professors are more productive than male full professors in education, physical sciences, and social sciences. Assistant professors among married women are the least productive. This may result in part from their younger age and accompanying familial status: that is, married assistant professors are more likely to have young children, a possible barrier to scholarly productivity. The fact that, among single women, full professors tend to be less productive could result from greater administrative responsibility, since a higher proportion of single than married women have administrative responsibilities.

TABLE 8.3

Productivity in Last Two Years by Rank, Sex, and Field
(percent)

Field	Professor			Associate Professor			Assistant Professor		
	Single Women	Married Women	Men	Single Women	Married Women	Men	Single Women	Married Women	Men
Education	13	41	26	22	31	43	11	24	28
Biology	24	47	57	22	44	56	24	36	54
Physical sciences	13	68	46	20	34	51	32	6	40
Social sciences	21	61	46	35	37	47	22	29	34
Humanities	20	42	43	19	30	20	22	14	13

Note: Productivity means three or more publications during the last two years.
Source: Compiled by the author.

When we do not control for rank and period of time men are more productive than women. However, married women are more productive than single women and men in some fields when rank is controlled. Differences in overall productivity among the three groups could result from differences in educational and work characteristics (Table 8.4). Examining the distribution of the three groups with respect to type of research they have engaged in, we find that in some ways married women more closely resemble men in these types of research. An examination of stipends during training indicates that a higher proportion of married than of single women had been teaching assistants or research assistants or had held fellowships or scholarships at some point. However, more of the men than of the women had had stipend support of some sort during graduate training.

An examination of the percentages of women and men who have attended high-quality undergraduate and graduate institutions revealed that 64 percent of the men received the B.A. and 80 percent the Ph.D. from high-quality institutions. Some 47 percent are currently teaching at high-quality institutions. For single women the percentages are 40 percent for a B.A. institution, 76 percent for a Ph.D. institution, and 38 percent currently teaching at a high-quality institution. Among married women the percentages are 49 percent for B.A. institution, 77 percent for Ph.D. institution, and 43 percent currently teaching at a high-quality institution. Again, we find that married women are more similar to men than to single women with respect to the quality of their training institutions and institutions of current employment.

TABLE 8.4

Educational and Work Characteristics
(percent)

	Single Women	Married Women	Men
Types of stipend while in training			
Teaching assistant	50	60	67
Research assistant	35	46	55
Scholarship or fellowship	65	72	70
Types of research engaged in*			
Pure	34	42	57
Applied	33	34	43
Policy	7	14	14
Literary	19	7	12

*These categories do not represent mutually exclusive responses. The sample was asked to indicate all responses that applied.

Source: Compiled by the author.

The differences between married and single women in stipend support and experiences, research activities, and quality of training institution might be in part the factors that can explain the higher productivity of married women. Married women also differ from single women in specialization (Table 8.5). For example, among married women, 26 percent are in social sciences, compared with

18 percent of the single women. Some 37 percent of the married women are in humanities, compared with 31 percent of the single women. However, a higher proportion of single women are specialized in education: 18 percent, compared with 9 percent of the married women.

TABLE 8.5

Distribution of Faculty, by Sex and Field
(percent)

Field	Single Women		Married Women		Men	
	N	Percent	N	Percent	N	Percent
Education	1,254	19	544	9	6,470	6
Biology	827	12	600	10	15,830	14
Physical sciences	565	8	507	7	25,730	22
Social sciences	1,199	18	1,520	26	22,420	19
Humanities	2,112	31	2,164	37	26,420	23
Other fields	784	12	581	10	20,640	18
Total all fields	6,741		5,916		117,480	

Source: Compiled by the author.

Institutional affiliation is also a factor in productivity. Men are more likely to be employed at universities (Table 8.6), while women are found in higher proportions in two-year and four-year institutions, colleges of low selectivity, and predominantly black institutions.

Quality of institution is also a variable in scholarly productivity. A somewhat higher proportion of married women (16 percent) than of single women (13 percent) are affiliated with highly selective universities.

An assessment of whether married women are more involved in research as principal investigators or coprincipal investigators and whether this involvement could result in greater productivity indicated that this is not the case. Where 34 percent of the men are not involved in grants or research contracts, 52 percent of the married women and 51 percent of the single women have no involvement. Furthermore, 33 percent of both married and single women hold the position of principal investigator on a research project, compared with 47 percent of the men.

TABLE 8.6

Distribution of Faculty, by Sex and Type of Institution
(percent)

Type of Institution	Single Women (N=6,741)	Married Women (N=5,916)	Men (N=117,480)
University, high selectivity	13	16	21
University, low selectivity	25	24	39
Four-year college, high selectivity	15	12	14
Four-year college, low selectivity	39	39	30
Two-year college	5	6	2
Predominantly black college	3	5	1

Source: Compiled by the author.

Do married and single women follow different career paths that could account for their differences in productivity? Table 8.7 lists previous employers for married and single women and men. Higher proportions of single women have come from teaching and administrative posts at the elementary and secondary level. However, more married women have been postdoctoral fellows or researchers in nonacademic settings. These differences in previous employment could account somewhat for the differences in productivity between married and single women.

Determinants of Productivity

In addition to the cross-tabulations used to examine productivity for single and married women and men by specialization, multiple

TABLE 8.7

Distribution of Faculty, by Sex and Previous Employment
(percent)

Previous Employment	Single Women (N=6,741)	Married Women (N=5,916)	Men (N=117,480)
Teaching in a university	22	22	31
Teaching in a four-year college	14	13	10
Teaching in a two-year college	2	3	1
Full-time nonteaching research	5	4	6
Postdoctoral fellowship	3	5	6
College or university administration	2	1	1
Teaching or administration in elementary or secondary school	13	7	2
Research outside educational institution	4	6	9
Administration outside educational institution	1	2	3
Other professional position	4	6	4
Student	26	24	24
Other	2	4	2

Source: Compiled by the author.

145

regression analyses were performed separately for the three groups. Multiple regression analysis permits one to observe the interrelationships among the factors that are relevant to productivity. Furthermore, the R multiple correlation provides information about the extent to which we can explain the variance in the criterion (productivity) on the basis of personal and environmental factors.

The criterion variables in the multivariate analysis were whether a person had published one or more articles versus none and one or more books versus none. The predictor variables for the regression analysis included educational background variables, current experiences, and characteristics of current institution. Specifically, the predictor variables were rank; ten fields representing the specialization and scored as dummy variables (business, education, biology, physical sciences, engineering, social sciences, fine arts, humanities, health fields, and other professions); and three dummy variables indicating whether the person had been a research assistant, a teaching assistant, or holder of a fellowship or scholarship. Additional variables included past work experiences: was the person, before coming to the current institution, affiliated with a university or a two- or four-year college? Was he or she employed in elementary or secondary education? Was the person an executive in a nonacademic setting or employed in a full-time nonteaching research position in a college or university? Background characteristics included father's and mother's education, race (white, black, Oriental), and age. For men, a variable indicating whether the person was married was included. Whether the person had children was a variable for all three subpopulations. Four additional variables describing the research in which the faculty member was engaged, such as pure, applied, policy, or literary, were also included. In addition to these personal and background characteristics, institutional variables were also utilized: whether it was a men's, a women's, or coeducational institution; whether it was private or public; and whether it was white or predominantly black. Geographic location was also identified. Three variables reflected institutional quality: the person's undergraduate or bachelor's institution, the institution from which the person received the highest degree, and the institution of current affiliation. *

Because the sample included only holders of a Ph.D., 72 percent of the sample population were affiliated with universities.

---

*Quality was a measure devised by Allan M. Cartter to reflect general faculty visibility, institutional affluence, and selectivity of students (Cartter 1975).

Almost a third were located in northeastern institutions. About 4 percent were affiliated with men's colleges and about 7 percent with women's colleges.

The predictors of productivity with respect to articles (one or more versus none published) were examined for each group, as well as the predictors of productivity with respect to books (one or more versus none published). For all the analyses, the variables entered freely by their predictive value except for rank, which entered last.

The regression analysis for article production by men (Table 8.8) revealed that the predictors, in order of importance, are: teaching in a university, doing pure research, having the highest degree in biology, and being affiliated with a high-quality institution. Having the highest degree in physical sciences also entered the regression analysis with a significant weight. In terms of other institutional characteristics that affect productivity, persons employed at institutions in the Northeast tend to be more productive than those affiliated with institutions in other regions. Men teaching at single-sex institutions, whether a women's or a men's college, are more productive than men teaching in coeducational institutions.

Men who were research assistants and who had a fellowship or scholarship at some point are more productive than those who did not have similar stipend support. A research assistantship has some direct relationship in that a person who was involved in research early is likely to develop tools useful in doing research later. Furthermore, a research assistantship and a fellowship or scholarship suggest that the person was awarded such stipends because of special abilities, accomplishments, or motivation.

An examination of the predictors for single women with respect to articles published (Table 8.9) indicated that being involved in pure or applied research is important. Additional variables indicated that the higher the quality of the current institution, the more likely the woman is to be productive. However, women teaching at institutions in the South are less likely to be productive. Fields also entered as predictors of publications, with biological and physical sciences carrying the largest weight, followed by health fields and social sciences. If a single woman has a fellowship or scholarship during her training, she is more likely to be productive later. The quality of the institution at which a woman receives her highest degree is also a factor in her productivity.

Where a single woman was previously employed is important to her overall productivity: if she was with a university, she is much more likely to have published. As indicated earlier, an affiliation with a university has added benefits, since universities have facilities and faculty there are expected to engage in scientific and scholarly writing.

TABLE 8.8

Predictors of Men's Productivity, Measured
by Published Articles

Predictor	Zero-Order Correlation	Beta Coefficient	F-ratio
Rank	+.17	+.179	36.26
Teaching in a university	+.18	+.136	27.29
Doing pure research	+.13	+.100	16.15
Highest degree in biology	+.10	+.098	15.88
Cartter quality,* current institution	+.18	+.089	13.72
Highest degree in physical sciences	+.08	+.090	12.96
Teaching at institutions in Northeast	+.03	+.070	8.74
Teaching at men's college	+.01	+.068	8.60
Teaching at a private institution	-.06	-.062	6.12
Highest degree in health field	+.04	+.054	5.91
Doing policy research	+.05	+.058	5.83
Scholarship in graduate school	+.06	+.054	5.60
Teaching at women's college	+.02	+.052	4.67
Doing applied research	+.07	+.052	4.52
Research assistantship in graduate school	+.12	+.045	3.61

*Cartter quality refers to a scale of 1 to 6 based on prestige rankings of institutions.
Note: R=.362. F=14.35.
Source: Compiled by the author.

Age is also a factor: the older the woman, the more likely she is to have been productive. Of course, age to some extent reflects the time a person has had to be productive.

The analysis with married women highlighted some additional predictors of scholarly productivity (Table 8.10). Besides rank, the most important is whether the woman had a fellowship or scholarship while training. Teaching at a women's college carries a negative weight. It is difficult to explain why affiliation with a women's college correlates with a married woman's low productivity.

Possibly married women affiliate with women's colleges because of marital constraints on their career advancement. Or perhaps married women who view their professional lives as secondary choose women's colleges, where the rewards might be greater for teaching than for research and publishing; thus their overall productivity is minimal. Without a better understanding of a woman's personal orientation, it is hard to attribute her low productivity to institutional effects.

TABLE 8.9

Predictors of Single Women's Productivity,
Measured by Published Articles

Predictor	Zero-Order Correlation	Beta Coefficient	F-ratio
Rank	+.21	+.176	23.30
Doing pure research	+.19	+.154	22.44
Doing applied research	+.13	+.133	17.70
Cartter quality,* current institution	+.20	+.124	16.42
Highest degree in biology	+.16	+.146	16.39
Highest degree in physical sciences	+.08	+.105	10.18
Teaching at institutions in the South	-.09	-.094	10.11
Scholarship in graduate school	+.12	+.081	6.82
Highest degree in health field	+.07	+.074	6.07
Age	+.13	+.088	5.69
Previous job in university	+.10	+.063	4.46
Highest degree in social sciences	+.08	+.073	4.28
Cartter quality,* highest degree institution	+.13	+.055	3.24

*Cartter quality refers to a scale of 1 to 6 based on prestige rankings of institutions.
Note: R=.447.   F=16.94.
Source: Compiled by the author.

TABLE 8.10

Predictors of Married Women's Productivity,
Measured by Published Articles

Predictor	Zero-Order Correlation	Beta Coefficient	F-ratio
Rank	+.24	+.214	31.46
Scholarship in graduate school	+.15	+.142	18.14
Teaching at women's college	-.13	-.126	15.70
Highest degree in humanities	-.18	-.117	10.89
Doing pure research	+.17	+.103	9.00
Cartter quality,* current institution	+.15	+.088	7.23
Previous job in elementary/ secondary school	-.13	-.076	5.37
Previous job in university	+.08	+.070	4.60
Previous job in four-year college	+.02	+.069	4.44
Previous job in nonteaching research	+.10	+.068	4.40
Highest degree, other professional	-.05	-.066	4.40
Race, black	-.08	-.065	4.24
Doing applied research	+.08	+.070	4.21
Highest degree in business	-.06	-.064	4.06
Cartter quality,* institution of highest degree	+.11	+.056	3.03

*Cartter quality refers to a scale of 1 to 6 based on prestige rankings of institutions.
Note: R=.448. F=12.03.
Source: Compiled by the author.

Pure and applied research both predict productivity with respect to published articles. Married women affiliated with high-quality institutions are more likely to publish more articles, a finding similar to that for single women. It is difficult, however, to know the extent to which the institutional environment causes higher productivity; perhaps productive women are simply more likely to affiliate with more visible institutions.

Whereas being at a university before coming to the present institution is a predictor of high productivity for single women, for married women either a university or a four-year college as a prior employer contributes to overall productivity. An additional important predictor for married women is whether they have been in a nonteaching full-time research position in an academic setting. Those in the humanities are less productive. Being in the biological sciences carries a small weight for married women compared with single women, for whom it is one of the most important predictors.

Comparing all three groups, men, single women, and married women, the common predictors of productivity as measured by published articles are being engaged in pure or applied research, having a degree in biology, quality of the current institution, and having a fellowship or scholarship while in graduate school. Comparing single women with men, the common predictors are having the highest degree in physical sciences or in health fields. Other than the common predictors for all three groups, there are no additional common predictors for men and married women. Comparing single women with married women, the common predictors are age, having a previous job at a university, and the quality of the highest degree-granting institution.

In addition to common predictors, there are some unique predictors for each of the three groups: for men, these are current institution, being at a university in the Northeast, being engaged in policy research, having a research assistantship, and being married. For single women, having the highest degree in social sciences is a unique positive predictor, with teaching at a southern institution a negative predictor. For married women, being at a women's college is a unique negative predictor, but having done research earlier or having been associated with a four-year college or a university is a positive predictor.

Analyses for the second measure of productivity, whether a person has published one or more books versus none, were performed separately for the three groups. An examination of the variables that separate men who have published books from those who have not (Table 8.11) indicated that, besides rank, the strongest predictor is the quality of the current institution. The question of cause and effect still remains: does being a productive person qualify one to be recruited and hired by a high-quality institution, or does affiliation with a high-quality institution affect productivity? Both conditions are plausible.

People engaged in applied research are just as productive with respect to books as to articles. Those in the natural sciences are much more likely to produce articles. Those in the physical sciences, engineering, or biological sciences are less likely to publish books than those in education and the humanities. Both policy and literary research entered the regression analysis as positive predictors of productivity for books.

TABLE 8.11

Predictors of Men's Productivity,
Measured by Published Books

Predictor	Zero-Order Correlation	Beta Coefficient	F-ratio
Rank	+.33	+.237	68.48
Cartter quality,* current institution	+.15	+.137	40.11
Doing applied research	+.11	+.098	16.96
Highest degree in physical sciences	-.14	-.109	16.63
Age	+.28	+.114	15.12
Highest degree in engineering	-.07	-.089	13.72
Doing policy research	+.14	+.082	12.47
Highest degree in biology	-.05	-.085	11.44
Teaching at institution in West	+.03	+.055	6.69
Highest degree in education	+.08	+.058	6.49
Race, black	-.02	-.055	5.86
Highest degree in humanities	+.11	+.066	5.67
Highest degree in business	+.07	+.050	5.36
Previous job in elementary/ secondary school	+.06	+.048	5.05
Children	-.06	-.043	4.03
Doing literary research	+.11	+.047	3.97
Teaching in black institution	+.03	+.042	3.55
Scholarship in graduate school	+.01	+.039	3.19

*Cartter quality refers to a scale of 1 to 6 based on prestige rankings of institutions.
Note: R=.459.   F=24.12.
Source: Compiled by the author.

Faculty men teaching in the West are more likely to publish books. Black men are less likely to publish books, unless they are teaching at black institutions. Having a scholarship or a fellowship while training entered the analysis as a predictor for books.

Examining the predictors of productivity for single women with respect to published books (Table 8.12) revealed that having the highest degree in biology or the physical sciences is a negative predictor, similar to the situation for men. Teaching at a university is a positive predictor. Again, it is hard to interpret this finding. As with men, the quality of the current institution is also a predictor of productivity. Engaging in pure research predicts high productivity. An unexpected finding was the negative relationship of quality of institution of highest degree and productivity in terms of books. Single women who received their Ph.D.s from selective institutions are less likely to publish books. For men exposure to a selective institution provides increased motivation, contacts, and important role models, but for women the case is apparently just the opposite. Without further investigation into the characteristics of the women who attend such institutions and their experiences, it is difficult to interpret the negative relationship.

TABLE 8.12

Predictors of Single Women's Productivity,
Measured by Published Books

Predictor	Zero-Order Correlation	Beta Coefficient	F-ratio
Rank	+.30	+.258	49.53
Highest degree in biology	-.12	-.162	26.70
Teaching at a university	+.15	+.145	20.62
Highest degree in physical sciences	-.10	-.106	12.41
Cartter quality,* institution of highest degree	-.02	-.104	11.36
Cartter quality,* current institution	+.12	+.102	10.19
Age	+.24	+.104	7.87
Doing pure research	-.02	+.075	5.57

*Cartter quality refers to a scale of 1 to 6 based on prestige rankings of institutions.
Note: R=.409.   F=24.05.
Source: Compiled by the author.

A married woman teaching at a women's college is less likely to publish books (Table 8.13). If she has her highest degree in biology or physical sciences, she is also less likely to publish books. However, if she had a scholarship or fellowship, she is more likely to publish books. Teaching at an institution in the South is a negative predictor, but being involved in applied, pure, or policy research is a positive predictor. The quality of current institution is a positive predictor.

TABLE 8.13

Predictors of Married Women's Productivity,
Measured by Published Books

Predictor	Zero-Order Correlation	Beta Coefficient	F-ratio
Rank	+.33	+.230	37.59
Age	+.29	+.184	22.53
Teaching at women's college	-.14	-.129	17.01
Highest degree in biology	-.07	-.124	13.76
Highest degree in physical sciences	-.08	-.098	9.50
Scholarship in graduate school	+.04	+.093	8.22
Teaching at institution in South	-.09	-.084	7.11
Doing applied research	+.11	+.079	5.72
Doing pure research	+.03	+.075	4.92
Previous job at four-year college	+.05	+.070	4.91
Cartter quality,* current institution	+.09	+.068	4.54
Highest degree in engineering	+.07	+.066	4.44
Doing policy research	+.13	+.069	4.36
Previous job in research	+.05	+.065	4.12

*Cartter quality refers to a scale of 1 to 6 based on prestige rankings of institutions.

Note: R=.461.   F=15.73.

Source: Compiled by the author.

Thus an examination of the common predictors for published books for all three groups indicated that the quality of current institutions is a most important predictor. However, it is difficult to ascertain whether being at a high-quality institution enables one to be productive, or whether being productive has helped one associate with an institution of high quality. Those in biology or physical sciences are less likely to write books. There are no common predictors for published books for men and single women, but there are some common predictors for men and married women. Being engaged in applied or policy research is a positive predictor. For single and married women, being engaged in pure research is an important predictor of productivity. A unique predictor for men is location of current institution: being in the West is a positive predictor. Having a degree in education, humanities, or business is positive, as is having a previous job in elementary or secondary education and being engaged in literary research.

For single women being affiliated with a university is a positive predictor. For married women being at a women's college is a negative predictor. Affiliation with a southern institution is also a negative predictor. Married women previously in nonteaching research positions tend to be more productive.

SUMMARY

In summary, whether productivity is expressed in published articles or books, one variable that appears to make a difference is field of specialization: the biological and physical sciences are important predictors of published articles, whereas humanities and education are important predictors of published books. The type of institution is an important variable: being at a university and at a high-quality institution are both important predictors, or at least are variables associated with high productivity. For married women, a former nonteaching research position predicts productivity. In the past, married women were less likely to receive academic appointments in institutions where their husbands were employed because of antinepotism regulations. Thus these women were often affiliated with research institutes and centers where their primary activity was research, leading to higher productivity rates.

The stipend support one has while training affects later productivity: a research assistantship appears to affect men and married women positively, while a teaching assistantship affects married women negatively. However, having a fellowship or scholarship affects all three groups in positive ways.

These analyses have also highlighted some interesting differences in career paths not only between men and women but also between married and single women. Contrary to current folklore, which maintains that the academic careers of single women resemble those of men more closely than do the careers of married women, the present study demonstrates that the careers of men and married women are actually more similar with respect to educational preparation, field of study, and publications. Thus the earlier writings by Lester (1974) and Sowell (1975) that tended to attribute the academic women's lower status to the constraints of marriage and family life do not necessarily hold true. The research reported in this chapter does not support that assumption. Examining the scholarly productivity of single and married women indicated that married women are more productive than single women. In some instances identical variables account for a married woman's and a man's productivity. One cannot conclude from this investigation that the careers of single women are more like those of men than those of married women, nor can one conclude that the lower status of academic women results from marital and family constraints.

Furthermore, the findings that productivity among married women increases dramatically with rank suggests that judging a married woman's potential on the basis of her performance when she is an assistant professor might not do justice to her potential for future scholarship and contributions in the field.

REFERENCES

Astin, H. S. The Woman Doctorate in America. New York: Russell Sage Foundation, 1969.

Astin, H. S. , and Bayer, A. E. "Sex Discrimination in Academe." Educational Record 53 (1972): 101–18.

Bayer, A. Teaching Faculty in Academe: 1972–1973. Washington, D.C.: American Council on Education, 1973.

Bayer, A. , and Astin, H. S. "Sex Differentials in the Academic Reward System." Science 188 (1975): 796–802.

Bernard, J. Academic Women. University Park, Pa. : Pennsylvania University Press, 1964.

Cartter, A. M. , and Ruhter, W. E. "The Disappearance of Sex Discrimination in First Job Placement of New Ph.D.'s." Los Angeles, Calif.: Higher Education Research Institute, 1975.

Crane, D. "Scientists at Major and Minor Universities: A Study of Productivity and Recognition." American Sociological Review 30 (1965): 699–714.

Folger, J., Astin, H. S., and Bayer, A. Human Resources and Higher Education. New York: Russell Sage Foundation, 1970.

Fulton, O., and Trow, M. "Research Activity in American Higher Education." Sociology of Education 47 (1974): 29–73.

Ladd, E. C., Jr., and Lipset, S. M. "Sex Differences in Academe." Chronicle of Higher Education 12 (1976): 18.

Lester, R. Antibias Regulation of Universities. New York: McGraw-Hill, 1974.

Science Citation Index. Philadelphia: Institute for Scientific Information, 1961, 1964, 1965.

Simon, R., Clark, S., and Galway, K. "The Woman Ph.D.: A Recent Profile." Social Problems 15 (1967): 221–36.

Sowell, T. Affirmative Action Reconsidered. Was It Necessary in Academia? Washington, D.C.: American Enterprise Institute for Public Policy Research, 1975.

Startup, R., and Gruneberg, M. "The Rewards of Research." Universities Quarterly 30 (1976): 227–38.

PART II

9
Intellectual Quality:
the Symbols and the Substance
Hilde E. Hirsch
Werner Z. Hirsch

In academic life there is an overriding concern with excellence,
with the intellectual quality of individual scholars and their work.
In addressing the issues of quality and the symbols and surrogates
used to indicate and measure it, one can define quality as the intellect, the depth and breadth of knowledge; the creativity to use this
intellect and knowledge to advance scholarship, ideas, art, or
science; and the ability to impart knowledge to others. The symbols
of quality, then, are those things that usually constitute a curriculum
vitae: a list of degrees and granting institutions (how prestigious),
positions held, papers and books published (where or by whom),
offices in professional associations, positions on boards and committees (editorial and governmental), honorary degrees, prizes,
and so on.

Rosemary Park is rich in both the symbols and substance.
She is of a tradition and a time in which intellectual quality was
appraised by the careful and deliberate judgment of those who most
highly prized and possessed it. In the last decade, however, painstaking contemplative assessment of scholarly and scientific merit
has increasingly been replaced by considerations of objectivity,
measurability, and time saving. Perhaps because of the explosive
rate at which university faculties have grown and published, old-
fashioned methods of evaluation have become too time-consuming
and cumbersome; transaction costs, in the economists' terms, have
become too high. In place of careful individual assessment, effi-
cient signals are sought. However, the price of overreliance on
signals and symbols may be not only that the symbols do not measure
quality as accurately, but also that they become ends in themselves,
surrogate goals; and in this rests a threat to scholarship and excellence.

Social scientists must share much of the blame. In their
work, which frequently necessitates measuring that which is essentially unquantifiable, they are forced to adopt the best available

numerical indicator even though they realize that as a measure of quality such an indicator is a particularly poor substitute for a true measure of quality. Administrators and deans, pressed for time and defensible decisions, tend to follow suit. In place of inquiring, painstaking reviews of scholarly and scientific performance, universities increasingly engage in a numbers game. Evaluation tends to stress quantity rather than quality; that is, the number of publications per year or the frequency with which an author's work is cited in the Citation Index, rather than the intellectual or practical importance of the contribution and its originality.

The use of surrogates by social scientists may be appropriate when they merely seek to describe and explain past events. Thus, for example, ex post research efforts rely on proxies that, on the average, may well correlate in a statistical sense with the characteristics to be evaluated. Such surrogates are amply justified to analyze the workings of institutions or to compare the productivity of one group with that of another, particularly where there are no other methods for objective evaluations. However, the picture is entirely different in assessing the achievement or potential of an individual scholar, especially when the task is to predict an individual's future contributions. For such purposes, surrogates should be treated with caution.

Nonetheless, many universities today are relying more and more on shortcuts, and the trend will probably continue because the shortcuts save time and are less susceptible to accusations of bias. Thus, for example, if a scholar's excellence is related to productivity, measuring productivity by numbers of publications is a great timesaver. The importance of a scholar's contribution is quickly assessed and compared with others by a glance at the Citation Index. This index, which lists all citations to an author's work, was even used in court to compare the academic standing of three professors at the University of Pennsylvania. When objective measures are so speedy and close at hand, can there be a doubt that they will be used increasingly in preference to the search for assessment by the most outstanding scholars in a narrow field who might, in due time, give their opinions? Is it not much easier to look through a curriculum vitae and compare, among other things, the prestige of institutions attended, even when evaluating a scholar 15 or 20 years after graduation?

If the case for increasing importance of surrogate quality indicators does not seem persuasive, consider the early stages of a selection process where all but the finalists are culled out. The criteria used at that stage are invariably symbolic in nature. For example, a department has a choice between two candidates for an associate professorship: the better qualified of the two by all criteria is unable to travel much because of an otherwise minor handicap. The inability to travel will prevent this candidate (many departments will reason) from attaining the visibility in the affairs of the discipline which would enhance the prestige of the department. The department is therefore likely to pass over the best qualified candidate, opting for the symbols of excellence over the reality.

The question is, of course, whether the signals commonly used reflect accurately what they are supposed to indicate. In a statistical sense it can be shown that they do on the average. But with regard to the individual, even if, on the average, the signals do not miss the mark, how often can one afford to miss an Albert Einstein (who until rather late in his career would have scored rather low on many present-day criteria) and appoint someone who was more active in professional societies, served on more boards, and published more papers?

Where the individual is concerned, many signals do not reflect quality accurately. Productivity is not a matter of numbers but of ideas; citations are most easily come by if a work forces other scholars to refute it and are, in any case, more a reflection of the momentary interest in an area of research than of the merit of a particular contribution. A telling case in point: the most frequently cited paper in the history of science is regarded by its author, O. H. Lowry of the Washington University School of Medicine, as "a scientific potboiler" much inferior to his other, less known contributions.

Are those who use these methods of evaluation sufficiently aware of the differences between certain areas of research which make it possible for some to publish dozens of papers per year, where others must labor long and hard for each contribution? Do they realize that in many of the hard sciences a book is not necessarily a more important piece of scholarly work than an article? Have they developed methods to account for the different meanings attached to coauthorship of papers in different fields--for example, in physics compared with the humanities?

Offices in professional societies tend today to go to those who have the time and the temperament to be active in such groups, not, as formerly, to a leading scholar, as an honor reflecting the esteem of professional peers. Thus where too much reliance is placed on symbols, they may often mislead.

In particular, women and minorities are likely to suffer from a reliance on surrogates that often poorly reflect true ability. Women are likely to lag behind men in position achieved x years after the Ph.D., number of publications, offices in professional associations, honorary degrees, and so on. There are a number of reasons for this: for example, during the period they are raising a family many women do not devote as much time to their job as men do. They may also be behind because this is still a man's world. The reason is certainly not intellectual inferiority. One can agree with Rosemary Park when she quotes Plato to the effect that "the same education which makes a man a good guardian will make a woman a good guardian; for their original nature is the same." In graduate school women are as competent as men, a fact documented by the Carnegie Commission on Higher Education (1973, p. 92). However, women may encounter various obstacles as well as discrimination, and their lists of qualifying signals tend to be shorter than those of a man of equal ability.

Incorrect reading of academic potential and achievement is particularly pernicious and harmful to women today, where many institutions of higher learning are in a steady state. Few positions are open, and competition for jobs between men and women is especially fierce. The present high level of unemployment further exacerbates this problem. Therefore, any built-in biases that stack the deck against women in the selection process must be avoided.

The issue of correctly identifying excellence where it exists applies to all groups. Not only the individual whose talent many go unrecognized and undeveloped, but also the general society suffers when superior minds are wasted. For this reason the present trend is potentially dangerous. But there is also another, more pernicious danger: the symbols are beginning to be sought, not for what they represent--proof of one's success as a scholar--but for themselves, because they bring success.

This trend leads to a decline of meticulous research as people aim for greater numbers of publications. In the years 1968-75, federal support for the basic sciences declined 23 percent; the number of journal articles published, however, increased from 1969 to 1976 by 13 percent, according to the National Science Foundation (1968-76, p. 4). During the same period, technical reports rose from 33,000 to 68,000. In other words, less research support resulted in more publications. Increasingly, papers are planned with an eye to the citations that will follow an intriguing title or sensational claims. Citing someone's work is often regarded as a favor. In some professional societies, scholars engage in unseemly campaigns to win offices. Graduate students approach professors for advice not on whether they have what it takes to pursue scholarship in the field, but on how to play the game for a successful career. Should such trends continue?

The time has come to weigh anew the advantages that go with using the shortcuts of symbols and signals with their relatively low transaction costs against the potential damage they may do. Distorted signals affect the selection and reward system, which may particularly harm women and minorities and lead to a waste of talent; they also provide incentives inimical to the advances of science and scholarship.

Society must guard against excessive inroads by numerical substitute criteria and protect the time-consuming system of personal evaluation and peer review, despite its potential for bias, pique, and jealousy, to preserve a judicious balance between the two. An editor of a good scholarly journal will submit a paper for review to some of the people cited in the reference list. That is perhaps the fairest system yet devised, particularly if the name and institution of the paper's author is omitted. In turn, the journal or publisher becomes a relatively good indicator of a paper's quality, and the sum of an author's work thus reflects the evaluations of many who are most familiar with his or her area. The same holds true of grants awarded under the peer review system. For example, the National Science Foundation charges its program administrators with selecting reviewers who are biased neither for nor against the candidate. Thus articles published in good journals and grants received can constitute valid signals. However, whenever possible, prominent scholars in the narrow area of interest should be asked their opinion. And scholars must be willing to give more time than they now do when asked for evaluations, or they will contribute to the erosive trend. Evaluation should be an honor rather than a chore.

Scholars must remember that productivity, as measured in numbers, is not necessarily good. Large numbers of citations can be more easily achieved by publishing a minor but time-saving variation on a widely used method than by a contribution that has an impact. Positions on committees may reflect personality traits that have nothing to do with scholarship. These indicators are acceptable for social science studies, but not when they become surrogate goals that do not coincide with the values of excellence in scholarship. In the long run, the effect of allowing the signals to become incentives can only be detrimental to excellence.

REFERENCES

Carnegie Commission on Higher Education. Opportunities for Women in Higher Education. New York: McGraw-Hill, 1973.

Scientific Citation Index. Philadelphia: Institute for Scientific Information, 1961, 1964, 1965.

National Science Foundation. Annual Report. Washington, D.C., 1968-76.

10
Responsibility and Public Policy: Is It a Moral Question?

Alan Pifer
Avery Russell

The American ideal of equality has undergone dramatic evolution in the last two centuries. When Thomas Jefferson wrote the word equal in the Declaration of Independence, it is generally thought he meant equality under natural law and in the sight of God. He certainly did not interpret the democratic ideal to mean social, economic, or educational equality for all, however defined. Nor were the framers of the Constitution particularly concerned with the emancipation of black slaves or women. They did not state that all persons were entitled to equal treatment, irrespective of race, color, religion, or sex.

Yet this is precisely what the term equality has come to signify today, and with this broader interpretation has come increasing discomfort over the disparity between what we profess and the conditions we see in society. Quite simply, the people of this nation have realized they can no longer tolerate the fundamental contradiction between the ideal of equality and the denial in practice of equal treatment for all. Since 1970 the American commitment to equal treatment has been extended even further to include the obligation by institutions not only to eliminate artificial barriers to equality, but also to take affirmative action to overcome the legacies of the past. While this concept refers to employment practices and is still controversial, the idea of redressing wrongs of the past is accepted by many as a moral principle with wide applications.

The Carnegie Council on Policy Studies in Higher Education (1975) has pointed out that the historical record of many colleges and universities, as well as other segments of society, has been "grossly inadequate" in meeting the test of equal opportunity for women and minorities. Policies in employment, promotion, and pay have been discriminatory, leaving it to the federal government to generate reform that higher education has not developed on its own. Not only has higher education been caught in a morally and legally indefensible position but, said the council, it has also failed its own principles of finding merit wherever it could be found and rewarding it. Further, it has "impoverished its own performance by the neglect of large pools of potential academic performance" (p. 3).

Much of the overt, institutionalized discrimination against academic women is being corrected, and colleges and universities are making some progress in affirmative action to overcome inequalities, albeit under federal pressure. Certainly the full equality of women, as a matter of lip service at least, is given homage everywhere within higher education. Few would have the temerity to avow openly that women should not have equal treatment with men.

But the persistent disparity between principle and practice, between goals and realities, is in danger of giving the lie to equality between men and women in the academic community. Despite the ferment over affirmative action and the recent increases in the proportion of women qualifying for appointment and promotion at the lower levels of the academic ladder, the proportion of women in the top faculty and administrative ranks has declined slightly in the last two years. Salary differentials between male and female faculty members also seem to be widening.

The reasons for this situation are manifold and complex. Outright discrimination still exists despite laws against it, subtle expressions of bias against women are endemic, role conflicts are still taking their toll on women who aspire to an academic career, and, more particularly, an essentially male-styled system has made few adjustments to those life patterns of women that differ from traditional norms.

Historical forces have also been at work--forces that are seen as having a negative impact on the status of academic women. Women have not yet succeeded in overcoming the decline in their ranks during the post-World War II baby boom, when the number of women preparing to enter the academic labor market dropped dramatically. This period, moreover, coincided with the rise to preeminence of the research universities, where women faculty and administrators have generally been absent. According to Patricia Graham (1977) the unintended consequence of this trend has been the suppression of women in higher education.

Finally, institutions of higher education find themselves in a period of retrenchment in which both academic men and women are in increasingly heavy competition for the few available jobs. Those institutions most adversely affected by steady state conditions are the liberal arts colleges that have been among the largest employers of women faculty. Additionally, women have lost ground through the decrease in the number of women's colleges. The Carnegie Council on Policy Studies in Higher Education (1975) noted that, while women will still find it easier to obtain jobs in two- and four-year colleges than in unversities, their proportions could shrink at these institutions as men are forced to accept positions they would have spurned in the past. The Carnegie Council predicted that charges of reverse discrimination by majority males can be expected to grow in volume and intensity as the number of faculty openings declines between now and the early 1980s, and these charges will meet with widespread public support.

In 1965, when they had lower career aspirations, women could have been absorbed into academe with relative ease. Now, when so many are ready to take on significant careers, there are few opportunities. Despite affirmative action, colleges and universities find themselves under parallel pressures to retreat from a commitment to equal educational opportunity for all, to close ranks against competition from those formerly outside the mainstream of education, and to rationalize this retreat in the name of meritocracy, economy, and academic freedom.

The case for equality for women in higher education, it appears, must be made again and again, surrounded by the more difficult challenge of defining what, exactly, constitutes equal opportunity and treatment and what, in the face of continuing sex bias and negative historical forces, should be the institutional response for making equality a reality.

There are at least four concepts of equality as it applies to human status. First, equality can mean equal results for all persons, that is, in their condition and in their rewards, regardless of differences in ability or in contribution to the general welfare. Such egalitarianism in its purest form has probably never existed in human history. Certain societies have approached it in varying degrees, and attempts have been made to establish utopian communities based on this ideal. Within an educational community, one could imagine a situation in which every group or subgroup in society was proportionally represented and in which every member, whether faculty or administrator, was absolutely equal to every other member in lifestyle, income, and position or status in the institution. Although this concept of equality has made its contribution to political philosophy, it has never been in the mainstream of western democratic tradition or thought. No pluralistic democracy can assure equal results for everybody. This is not, therefore, the concept that applies to equality for women in higher education.

A second definition is formal equality of opportunity, wherein all persons are given a fair chance to succeed, in the sense that no arbitrary barriers are erected to inhibit their upward progress within an existing system. Since this definition takes no account of either inherited differences such as handicaps or advantages of birth or cultural differences, it leads almost inevitably to a society characterized by inequality. Nevertheless, its supporters claim validity on two grounds: first, because some individuals, despite formidable obstacles, do rise in social and economic position; and second, on the assertion that all people, regardless of class differences (which we do not like to acknowledge), are entitled to equal respect. This is the traditional concept of equal opportunity, although during much of this nation's history it has not applied to members of minority groups or women. In its current application to the treatment of women in higher education it has serious flaws. It assumes that the female scholar must be assimilated by a male-dominated institution and adopt conventional strategies for getting ahead, without accommodations in the existing system. While this may appear justified on the surface, in practice some academic women find that strict conformity to the established system may run afoul of the competing needs of marriage and family; others conform only to find their performance judged not on merit but by a double standard that favors men. As one female scholar put it: "You have to be better than a man if you are to be considered as good."

A third concept of equality involves a move toward conditions for competition through affirmative action. This means not only the elimination of artificial barriers to equal opportunity, but also the eradication of policies and practices that have discriminatory effects and the demonstration of good faith by efforts to redress past inequalities. Within higher education it means a broadening of criteria for entering the system, an active search for talent in those groups formerly discouraged from competition, special assistance to disadvantaged individuals, and the making of decisions without improper regard for sex, race, and ethnic origin. Affirmative action maintains that excellence exists across race, class, and sex, and that a diverse society requires a similar diversity among the professionals who serve it. Thus the concept is rooted not only in moral values, but also in the recognition of societal needs. The flow in affirmative action, however (as in any other framework for achieving equality), is that it does not require basic accommodation in a male-patterned system to the special qualities, values, and life patterns that women may bring to it. This is not an argument founded on the notion of a distinct women's culture, but on the simple recognition that women and men have been raised differently and that women, as childbearers, have often found themselves at a competitive disadvantage in the race with men to reach the pinnacles of professional life. Underlying these facts are still prevalent assumptions about the traditional roles, behaviors, and capacities of women which provoke subtle forms of bias just as pernicious in their effects as outright discrimination. So far, affirmative action has had little effect on these problems.

A fourth model for achieving equal opportunity goes further by posing a more cooperative system, one which, paradoxically, would lead to greater choice for the individual pursuing an academic career. Such a system would reflect the concerns of both men and women and would make adjustments to the obligations of family life shared equally by husband and wife. Traditionally the male scholar's family has been at the service of his needs; the female scholar, if she marries, has had no such support system. To the contrary, she has often been embattled by the opposing claims of career and family and finally forced to choose between the two. Jessie Barnard has commented that "there is something about the academic profession which makes it . . . inimical to marriage among women" (1964, p. 206). This may or may not be the case today, but indications that young women academics are delaying marriage or children until they have gained a foothold on the academic ladder do not prove that there is no longer any problem. The trends may suggest that, once again, the adjustment has been on the woman's side, not within the system.

Associated with the difficulties for women of a tradition-bound system of higher education are holdover beliefs by a predominantly male academic leadership that women are less intellectually able than men and that their careers cannot be taken as seriously. The notions that equate women's biological inheritance with mental inferiority, the cultivation of women's minds with their defeminization, or the intellectual woman with a neurotic or in some way deviant background are far from dead. Such cultural myths and prejudices serve even today to inhibit women's full participation in many public arenas. But if institutions of higher education were to inaugurate flexible policies that allowed rising female academics to have families without penalty to their careers and that encouraged men to pursue a career without subordinating the family, this tendency to undervalue the aspirations, experience, and creations of women might disappear.

Some flexible policies, such as permitting part-time appointments for women with families or enabling those who hold half-time jobs to achieve tenure, have been suggested or implemented. However, reforms may pose further dangers to women if women are seen as the primary beneficiaries: a kind of two-track system could develop in which part-timers--mostly women--would once again be at a competitive disadvantage. Policies must be carried out to involve men and women as equally as possible. To do this may require structural changes deep within the university system as well as within the family, with a new set of values that fully incorporates the experience and talent of both sexes.

Is there a moral basis for arguing that college and university administrators and faculties have a responsibility to change any attitudes, policies, and practices that result in differential effects for academic men and women? The answer is a resounding yes. Formal adherence to affirmative action regulations, even if that were achieved, cannot produce true equality of treatment for women if there is not true commitment to the spirit of the law. Confronting and banishing the subtle expressions of bias (whether intended or unconscious and introducing flexibility into the system to improve access are necessary to eliminate the disparity between dreams and reality.

The moral and ethical basis for this assertion is indisputable, for if the citizens of society say they believe in equality but still uphold conditions that militate against full and equal participation of women, they are in a hypocritical and morally untenable position. Moreover, higher education would be untrue to the standard of meritocracy if it were to neglect the pool of talent found in all groups in the population, talent that would enhance the richness and diversity of institutional offerings.

The ultimate justification for the special protection that society affords the college or university is the claim to morality which is intrinsic to its own mission to search for truth, no matter what the consequences. Truth, however, by its very nature, can be pursued only in an unfettered manner, and an institution that practices discrimination is compromising that search and forfeiting its claim to morality.

In sum, discrimination, however subtle or unconscious, is inescapably a moral flaw in the college or university, and it is this fact that makes equality for women in higher education a moral question.

REFERENCES

Bernard, J. Academic Women. University Park, Pa.: Pennsylvania State University Press, 1964.

Carnegie Council on Policy Studies in Higher Education. Making Affirmative Action Work in Higher Education. San Francisco: Jossey-Bass Publishers, 1975.

Graham, P. Personal communication. 1977.

11
Civil Rights and
the Women's Movement
Theodore M. Hesburgh

During recent years I have been severely criticized for being
forthrightly and enthusiastically in favor of the Equal Rights Amendment (ERA). It has been alleged that this puts me on the side of
those who are destroying womanhood in America. I guess that the
truth of the matter depends on what womanhood in America is perceived to be, either ideally or realistically. I am happy to declare
myself on that point, and will do so presently.

When asked to defend my support of ERA, I simply say that
the whole history of America has been the study of the enlargement
of justice for everyone. ERA is part of that development, long over-
due. During the Bicentennial year we heard the stirring words of
the Declaration of Independence: "We hold these truths to be self-
evident, that all men are created equal and are endowed by their
creator with certain unalienable rights, that among these are life,
liberty, and the pursuit of happiness."

Great words, but we were not often reminded that the Declaration of Independence merely declared these rights; it did not effect
them. In fact, when the words were written in 1776 and when, to
establish justice and secure these rights, the Constitution was written in 1789, those great human rights were fully enjoyed by only
affluent, mature, free, Anglo-Saxon men. The most fundamental
political right, voting, was not enjoyed by women in America until
this century by amendment of the Constitution in 1920. Must one
say that this is the result of prejudice? I would simply say yes,
prejudice and all its associated ills, especially clichés such as
"women are weak," "women are unstable and irrational," "women
shouldn't mix in politics," "woman's place is in the home, not the
political arena," "all women will simply vote like their husbands,"
and so on.

One could argue that the enjoyment of the full panoply of human
rights for women would follow the right to vote. One might just as
well claim that the problem of rights for blacks was solved by the

passage of the Thirteenth, Fourteenth, and Fifteenth Amendments following the Civil War. We still needed, a century later, the omnibus Civil Rights Act of 1964, the Voting Rights Act of 1965, and the Housing Act of 1968. Even now, the problem of basic human rights for blacks is far from a full solution. The same may be said for women: their struggle for equality is a long, arduous, uphill battle.

Inequality for women is an ancient tale. It took a woman, Rivkah Harris of Northwestern University, to point out recently that of the 185 scribes in the Babylonian city of Sippar, between 1850 and 1550 B.C., only ten were women. Scribes at that time happened to be highly honored professional people in a sea of illiteracy. They required long years of education. All one needed to qualify was intelligence and manual dexterity for writing complicated cuneiform characters on clay tablets. It is not surprising that although many women are endowed with high intelligence and manual dexterity, a preponderance of men was chosen for the honored positions, even that long ago. Prejudice, the enemy of equality and equal rights among men and women, has deep roots in history. Nothing that deeply rooted will be easily eradicated from the minds and hearts and attitudes of mankind. "All men are created equal." Men have tended to take that statement to mean literally and univocally all men.

One does not have to go back in history 3,500 years to demonstrate the necessity for concerted effort and cumulative legislation to balance a situation that is still completely out of balance today. However one views the women's movement today, a close look at the actual situation in America should persuade even the most prejudiced that women are discriminated against in many ways. The record speaks for itself. Women may, in fact, need a much more effective women's movement than they have if they are to enjoy equality of opportunity in the foreseeable future. A few men should also join the movement, for undoubtedly prejudice comes mainly from the male side.

Here are a few striking facts which I extracted from a 362-page report to President Ford by the National Commission on the Observance of International Women's Year:

Thirty-seven million American women work outside the home. White women's median earnings are $6,823, while the comparable figure for white men is $12,104. The black woman faces a double prejudice in achieving equality and justice. Black women receive a median salary of $6,258 compared with $8,524 for black men.

In elementary and secondary education, women represent 67 percent of all teachers, but only 15 percent of women are principals in elementary schools and only 3 percent of high schools have women principals.

Six million women belong to labor unions, but are almost completely without a voice in the management of unions. A most striking case is the International Ladies' Garment Workers Union, which has one "lady" on its 23-member board of directors. One word for that is tokenism; another is inequality.

Women make up 53 percent of the voting population and 39 percent of the labor force. Only 5 percent of women hold elective government positions. I spare you the percentage for lawyers, doctors, scientists, and engineers.

There are 399 authorized judgeships in the United States district courts and 97 judges in the federal appeals courts. Women judges in these courts number four, much less than 1 percent. In the 200-year history of our country only ten women have been named to the federal bench, none ever to the Supreme Court.

Jobs traditionally done by women are consistently undervalued in the federal governments' Dictionary of Occupational Titles, which is often used to determine salary levels. For example, dog trainers are rated higher than foster mothers. Paraprofessional jobs in education, health, and welfare are classified menial because they are generally performed by women.

Need I say more? It is not so much that this represents monumental injustice toward women, but it has a deleterious effect on the self-image, motivation, and hopes of young women who cannot expect equal opportunity or recompense, despite equal intelligence and education, not to mention equal or superior performance. In addition, the nation itself is deprived of much creativity and intelligence. This is a continuing and cumulative impoverishment that we can ill afford in America. To make the picture even more dismal, America looks like a paradise for women compared to most of the world beyond our shores. However, that does not justify our delay in living up to the promises of our Declaration of Independence and our Constitution, even if we have to amend the Constitution to speed up the process.

The situation of women in America may be one of the best reasons for reviewing the whole effort toward achieving civil rights in our day. I have been reasonably quiet on the subject since my quick dismissal by President Nixon immediately following his re-election in 1972. I had spent 15 years on the Commission on Civil Rights since its inception in 1957, the last four years as chairman. Those were golden years when America in the 1960s made great strides toward reversing the mores and practices that had humiliated blacks since the first days of slavery in our country. Enormous progress was made in establishing equality of access in public accommdations; segregation was practically eliminated overnight with the passage of the federal Civil Rights Act of 1964.

There was also an impressive breakthrough with the 1965 voting-rights law. Within a few years we went from a handful to thousands of elected black officials, including many members of Congress and the mayors of some of our largest cities across the nation: Washington, Newark, Detroit, Atlanta, and Los Angeles. There was also a massive increase in equality of opportunity for blacks in that concatenated and problematic trilogy of education, employment, and housing--the latter thanks largely to the federal fair-housing law of 1968, which had been filibustered to death a year earlier.

While all of this was happening to blacks (our largest minority, numbering more than all the Canadians in Canada), we of the Civil Rights Commission were concerned that forward progress was far slower on all fronts for Spanish-speaking Americans, mainly Mexican-Americans and Puerto Ricans, and, of course, almost no progress for native Americans. As we began to intensify our efforts on both of these other fronts in the late 1960s and early 1970s, the women's movement (previously quieter) began in earnest, and we suddenly realized that women were not specifically included in our legislative mandate which only cited race, religion, color, and national origin, the standard legal list of concerns for unequal protection of the laws in America.

A new and concerted effort was mounted on the part of the women's movement, in which we concurred and with which we collaborated enthusiastically. As a result, the basic 1957 law creating the Commission on Civil Rights was amended in the early 1970s to read "race, religion, color, national origin, and sex." There was some resistance, for some thought that our new involvement with the women's movement would dilute our efforts for the standard minorities. I said at the time and I still believe that the problem of equal rights for women, at least white women, would eventually be easier to solve than the problems relating to prejudice on account of color. Even so, one cannot be selective in fighting injustice. One must be against injustice wherever and whenever it is encountered. Justice, like truth and freedom, is indivisible. When one person suffers injustice, we should all suffer.

All of this leads me to two broader observations. First, I think that the time has come, even for the women's movement, to drop the term civil rights in favor of the broader and more comprehensive term human rights. It is a curious development that the western world of Europe and America has tended to emphasize in its political documents civil and political rights, while the socialist countries have spoken more frequently of economic, social, and cultural rights. When the Universal Declaration of Human Rights of the United Nations was reduced to political protocols for approval

by governments, there were two, following this same division of
political and civil rights in the one document and economic and social rights in the other.

I believe that we in America have come far enough in our recent developments to speak now of the whole panoply of rights--
political, civil, economic, social, cultural, religious, and educa-
tional--all of which would be contained in the one expression human
rights, now recognized worldwide (at least in principle) following
the almost universal acceptance of the United Nations Declaration
of Human Rights. Moreover, it seems to me that this larger expression is a felicitous elaboration of the phrase in our Declaration
of Independence, "the pursuit of happiness." It is unthinkable that
one could honestly pursue happiness or human fulfillment in modern
America without enjoying the whole spectrum of what might best be
called human rights.

My second observation is that we in America can no longer
just think of our own pursuit of happiness. Somehow our concern
for human rights here in America must be linked to the same concern for human dignity and human rights everywhere. I would, of
course, say the same for the concerns of the women's movement
here and abroad. The striving for women's rights should be worldwide, for whatever our problems for equality of women in America,
the problem is far worse in most of the rest of the world.

When one looks at the problems facing us today, it is quickly
evident that the worst of them are necessarily worldwide and interdependent in their understanding, as well as in their solution. Ultimately there are no purely national solutions for energy, hunger,
development, trade, terrorism, population, monetary systems,
use of the seas, environment, health, disarmament, peace, justice,
and human rights. In this increasingly interdependent world our
efforts must be both national and international. We breathe the
same air, we drink the same water, we are each of us passengers
on a single spaceship earth, with finite irreplaceable life resources,
with a common yearning for peace and justice. I suspect that we
will achieve our common hopes together or not at all.

Before abruptly departing from the Civil Rights Commission,
I had been urging my fellow commissioners to consider renaming
our work the Commission on Human Rights and enlarging our pur-
view to consider the human rights implications of everything the
United States does, not just nationally but worldwide. What, for
example, are the implications of a nation dedicated to and working
for liberty and justice for all but giving preferential aid treatment
and arms to repressive regimes that trample on the human rights of
their citizens, for example, in South Korea and Chile?

Two hundred years ago a small country of 3 million people spread thinly over 1,400 miles of Atlantic coastline in 13 very disparate colonies declared that all men were created equal, that its government was created to secure their rights, and that this government derived its just powers from the consent of the governed. In fact the world was never the same again, from the French Revolution that followed soon after our Declaration of Independence to the complete freeing of a vast colonial world which has happened in our lifetime. If I had one mandate for the women's movement today, it would be that they take their inspiration from our beginnings and dedicate themselves to making America today what Governor John Winthrop challenged the fledgling Massachusetts Bay Colony to become, a good city set upon a hill, for all the world to see.

I would hope that by now I have sufficiently established my dedication to the best of the women's movement to be indulged a word or two of criticism. It is no state secret that the passage of the ERA is presently in trouble. Even some states that have approved the amendment are now attempting to retract their approval. What went wrong? I think that somehow the women's movement, or at least its leadership, went astray, and in doing so estranged many women. Curiously, most of the criticism I receive for supporting ERA comes from women, not men. Women across the land are in the vanguard of efforts to defeat ERA, which somehow has become entangled with abortion, lesbianism, masculinizing women, destroying family stability, ambisextrous rest rooms, female combat service in the Armed Forces, and so on.

Somehow the whole essence of the movement, its deep meaning for feminine equality and identity, its inherent justice and rightness, have been lost in the process. My only advice is for women to get the whole movement back on the tracks going somewhere that most women want to go. I don't think that men can do it, even though they can and should collaborate.

As a Christian theologian, I am often heartened by the way that theology can point reality in the right direction when a good movement falters. Just consider two ancient texts, one Jewish, another Christian. They put the whole matter quite simply.

First, consider the story of creation in the opening chapter of the Book of Genesis, which is one of the first great statements on the relationship of men and women. It says that only in being men and women is mankind reflective of the image of God. There is no confusion here, as there is in "all men are created equal." It even specifies the best reason for human dignity and equality: together they reflect the image of God.

God said, "Let us make man in our own image, in the
likeness of ourselves, and let them be masters of the
fish of the seas, the birds of the heavens, the cattle, all
the wild beasts, and all the reptiles that crawl upon the
earth." God created man in the image of Himself, in
the image of God he created him, male and female he
created them. (Genesis 1:26-7, emphasis added)

The good news that Christ, Our Lord, brought into the world
was proclaimed by St. Paul to a world that was split (as ours is
yet) between nations, free men and slaves, men and women. Paul
proclaimed that these distinctions were less important than the
basic oneness and unity of human beings, especially those who are
one in Christ, something transcending our basic human oneness:
"All baptized in Christ, you have clothed yourselves in Christ, and
there are no more distinctions between Jew and Greek, slave and
free, male and female, but all of you are one in Christ Jesus"
(Galatians 2:27-8).
    Despite the grandeur of these texts, 2,500 years have not
sufficed to help us create a world that would reflect realistically
what they teach. In the thirteenth century even a great theologian
like Thomas Aquinas could repeat the assertion of the Greek
philosopher, Aristotle, who said that woman was a miscarried,
or incomplete, man. I often fight off discouragement by remem-
bering a conversation with the late French philosopher, Jacques
Maritain, who said that mankind's history is a long uphill growth
in moral discernment. Certainly the women's movement moves us
in that direction. There is a very special energy in women, an
energy seeking to be liberated for good. As another Frenchman,
the Jesuit anthropologist Teilhard de Chardin, said, "to limit
energy," to allow the treasury of feminine energy to be diluted or
lost, "that is sin." Following the inspiration of Genesis, Teilhard
also says to us about women, "Listen, it is God who awaits you in
me." They too, are in a very special way, God's image among us.
    On that note, I would like to make a few personal observations
about Rosemary Park, who has inspired all of the contributors to
this volume. I will try to relate what she is to what I have been
writing about.
    First, it must be said that Rosemary is quintessentially a
woman, a lady. She brings me back where I began, namely to what
womanhood in America today is. I cannot precisely detail all that
this means, but looking at Rosemary, I know what it is to be a
woman, to be something special that we men can never be. To be
with her is to be specially enriched in a most feminine way.

Best of all, she utterly destroys, just by being what she is, all the hackneyed stereotypes about women. She is highly intelligent and superbly educated, both here and in Europe. She speaks with the authority of one who has studied and read widely and knows exactly what she is talking about. She not only knows what to say, but also how to say it well and clearly. There is nothing weak or shy about her; she leads from the strength of a strong mind and deeply held convictions. But she does this in a very special way, not alienating people, but quietly convincing them with reason. What comes through is her confident competence. She has had an unusually rich professional experience in her varied lifelong tasks, and she has learned from what she has seen and lived, as well as from what she has read and studied.

Rosemary Park is not only a pleasant person but a woman of character, a lover of civilizing values, who lives what she loves. You know if you are her good friend, but I suspect that friendship with her depends largely on the kind of person you are. I suspect that she would not suffer fools gladly, at least not moral fools.

Because of her superb qualities, Rosemary Park has been called upon to perform at the highest levels of higher education. I suspect that hers has been largely a pioneering role, that of being the first woman to do this or that important task. Because she always performed so well, always essentially as a woman, the requests multiplied as the years passed. So her influence and her host of friends widened. All of us learned, through her, that we had missed a great deal over the years by not having more women like her to enrich our many associations. To know and to work with Rosemary Park was to grow in respect for the special leadership and creativity and insights that only a woman can bring to a wide variety of tasks that all too long have been essentially and solely performed only by men.

All of us who worked closely together monthly for six years on the Carnegie Commission on Higher Education were enriched by her presence and her friendship. In almost every important association, council, or commission for higher education, she made her presence felt, her ideas accepted, and her leadership acknowledged.

When the University of Notre Dame decided to become coeducational in 1972, it was obvious that we would only avoid serious difficulties if we could enjoy the insights that a talented woman educator could provide us. Fortunately, Rosemary Park was the first woman member of our board of trustees, the first of many, so valuable was her contribution. She had already served the university superbly in providing us with a basic study of the problems and opportunities involved in a possible merger with our sister institution, Saint Mary's College. As our university trustee, Rosemary quickly assumed chairmanship of a most important Faculty Affairs Committee, again the only woman among fellow trustees and elected faculty members on that committee. Once more, she performed outstandingly in a variety of difficult situations that simply could not have been handled as well by any man available. She proved to us all that a professional woman is a great unifying force, even among, perhaps especially among, embattled men.

What has all of this to do with the women's movement and human rights? Certainly women should not have to prove themselves any more than men to achieve equality as human beings in human affairs. However, that is at times, given the attitudes of our society, the only way that a vicious circle of prejudice is broken. It is difficult to argue against a fact, especially the fact of demonstrated intelligence, widespread competence, and deep personal influence, all demonstrated by a quintessential woman.

Rosemary Park has done all of this and more for many years. She has been a one-person women's movement all by herself. She has opened more doors than a battalion of noisy and abrasive women. In a recent discussion I attended, someone complained to Margaret Mead that some women had performed well without much notice. Margaret Mead responded with some acerbity, "But they didn't come through as women. They don't even look like women!"

No one will ever say that of Rosemary Park. She is proud to be a woman. She knows that a woman can do as a woman some very special tasks in a very special way. She has no desire to be a man, even to be competitive with men. She truly complements every men's group she joins. Her insights surprise them. Her understanding, compassion, and sensitivity make most men look like Neanderthals. Her intelligence and learning have a special edge that we men often need and lack.

We who have been blessed to work with her and love her cannot forget that special light in her eyes, sometimes soft but hard when needed, that special smile that so often dissolves opposition and welds affection. Thank God for Rosemary Park and women like her. We have much to learn from all they can teach us. My only problem with Rosemary is how we can possibly replace her when she retires. I am sure that she will say, "There are a million Rosemarys out there. You fellows just have not been looking hard enough." She will say it with such gaiety and charm that all of us fellows will try to believe her, but all the time we will know in our hearts that there is only one Rosemary Park. If there really were millions, we would not need a women's movement. Maybe that is the basic problem, and maybe as men, that is our fault.

Rosemary Park:
Professional Activities

At the same time that she was fully engaged in teaching and administration, Rosemary Park has been active in a large number of enterprises, both academic and civic.

She has been a member of the Opportunity Fellows Committee of Awards of the John Hay Whitney Foundation (1955-59); the Defense Advisory Commission--Women in the Services (1956-58); the General Motors National Scholar Committee (1960-63); the Commission on Independent Colleges and Universities of New York (1962-67); the Regents' Commission on Educational Leadership, New York (1964-67); the Selection Committee, Florina Lasker Civil Liberties Award (1965 and 1967); the Board of Visitors, Women's College, Duke University; the Citizens' Advisory Council; the Far West Laboratory for Educational Research and Development; the National Citizens' Committee for Public Television (1967); and the State Accreditation Board, Department of Education, state of California (1967-70). She was also a director of the Association of American Colleges; chairman (1965), the Rockefeller Brothers Theological Fellowship Program (1961-64); the American Council on Education (1963-66); the American Council on Emigrés in the Professions (1963-67); the Committee on Human Values in a Society of Advancing Technology for the National Council of Churches (1964-67); the Crowell-Collier and Macmillan Company (1965-69); and the Danforth Foundation (1966-72).

She is now a trustee of Scripps College, Claremont, California (1967-), the Marlborough School for Girls (1970-), and the Carnegie Council for Policy Studies in Higher Education, and was previously trustee of the Carnegie Foundation for the Advancement of Teaching, Notre Dame University, Robert College (Istanbul), St. John's College (Annapolis, Md.), Miss Porter's School (Farmington, Conn.), and the Masters School (Dobbs Ferry, N.Y.), the University of Hartford, and the Institute for International Education. She was president of the United Chapters of Phi Beta Kappa (1970-73) and remains senator-at-large (1961-). Radcliffe gave her the Graduate Chapter Medal (1961) and the Alumnae Award (1975), and she was honored as Woman of the Year by the Westchester County Federation of Women's Clubs (1963) and the Los Angeles Times (1968). She was elected fellow of the American Academy of Arts and Sciences in 1956.

While serving on the advisory council of the National Endowment for the Humanities she was chairman of the Research Committee, which had responsibility for the award of fellowships to scholars. Her principal concern was that worthy scholarly projects in the humanities and basic research should receive a fair proportion of the available funds.

She has received the following honorary degrees: Doctor of Literature: Claremont Graduate School (1972); LL.D: Wesleyan, Conn. (1948), Mt. Holyoke (1955), Rutgers (1956), Yale (1958), Massachusetts (1960), Bridgeport (1962), Brown (1962), Columbia (1962), N Y U (1962), Goucher (1963), Oberlin (1963), University of Pennsylvania (1964), University of Hartford (1965), Loyola, Chicago (1970), Notre Dame (1974), Syracuse (1965), Williams (1967); L.H.D.: Wheaton (1954), Woman's Medical College of Pennsylvania (1964), and Doctor of the University of Hartford (1959).

About the Editors
and Contributors

HELEN S. ASTIN is Professor of Higher Education, University of California at Los Angeles, and Vice-President, Higher Education Research Institute. A member of the American Psychological Association's Board for Policy and Planning, she has served previously as chairperson of the APA's Task Force on the Status of Women in Psychology and as President, Division 35 (Division of the Psychology of Women). A trustee of Hampshire College, Dr. Astin holds membership on the Board of Human Resource Data and Analyses of the National Research Council as well as on the editorial boards of the Journal of Counseling Psychology, Journal of Vocational Behavior, Psychology of Women Quarterly, Signs, and Sage Annuals in Women's Policy Studies. Her own publications include Human Resources and Higher Education; The Woman Doctorate in America; Women: A Bibliography on Their Education and Careers; Higher Education and the Disadvantaged Student; Open Admissions at CUNY; Sex Roles: An Annotated Research Bibliography; and The Power of Protest.

WERNER Z. HIRSCH is Professor of Economics, University of California at Los Angeles, and consultant to the RAND Corporation and the Organization for Economic Cooperation and Development. From 1953 to 1963 professor of Economics and director, Institute of Urban and Regional Studies, Washington University, St. Louis, he has served as a consultant to the National Science Foundation, the National Commission on Civil Disorders, the International Institute for Educational Planning, and the Senate Select Committee on the Structure and Administration of Public Education in California. Dr. Hirsch's publications include Analysis of Rising Costs of Public Education, Elements of Regional Accounts, Inventing Education for the Future, Spillover of Public Education Costs and Benefits, The Economics of State and Local Government, Program Budgeting for Primary and Secondary Public Education, Financing Public First-Level and Second-Level Education in the United States, Urban Economic Analysis, and Local Government Program Budgeting.

ALEXANDER W. ASTIN, Professor of Higher Education, University of California at Los Angeles.

MARGARET GORDON, Associate Director Carnegie Council on Higher Education, University of California, Berkeley.

REVEREND THEODORE M. HESBURGH, C.S.C., President of the University of Notre Dame.

HILDE E. HIRSCH, Research Neurologist, Department of Neurology and Reed Neurological Research Institute, University of California, Los Angeles School of Medicine.

SUSAN ROMER KAPLAN, Ph.D. Candidate, School of Education, University of California, Berkeley.

CLARK KERR, Chairman, Carnegie Council on Higher Education, Professor Emeritus of Economics and Industrial Relations, University of California, Berkeley.

C. ROBERT PACE, Professor of Higher Education and Director of Laboratory for Research on Higher Education, University of California at Los Angeles.

ALAN PIFER, President of the Carnegie Corporation of New York and of the Carnegie Foundation for the Advancement of Teaching.

ESTHER RAUSHENBUSH, President Emeritus, Sarah Lawrence College, Senior Associate Whitney Foundation.

AVERY RUSSELL, Executive Staff and Director of Publications, Carnegie Corporation.

SHEILA TOBIAS, Associate Provost, Wesleyan University.

Related Titles
Published by
Praeger Special Studies

COMPARATIVE PERSPECTIVES ON THE
ACADEMIC PROFESSION
                              edited by
                              Philip G. Altbach

MALE AND FEMALE GRADUATE STUDENTS:
The Question of Equal Opportunity
                              Lewis C. Solmon

SEX DISCRIMINATION IN CAREER COUNSELING
AND EDUCATION
                              Michele Harway
                              Helen S. Astin

WOMEN AND MEN: Changing Roles, Relationships,
and Perceptions
                              Libby A. Cater
                              Anne Firor Scott

WOMEN'S INFERIOR EDUCATION: An Economic
Analysis
                              Blanche Fitzpatrick

*WOMEN'S RIGHTS AND THE LAW: The Impact of
the ERA on State Laws
                              Barbara A. Brown
                              Ann E. Freedman
                              Harriet N. Katz
                              Alice M. Price

*Also available in paperback.